THIS TYPE OF SCENERY...
THIS SORT OF MOVIE...
THIS KIND OF COOKIE...

BARRON'S
E-Z
GRAMMAR

Dan Mulvey, M.A.

WESTCHESTER PUBLIC LIBRARY
3 1310 00248 3600

W9-BZT-140

Better Grades or Your Money Back!

As a leader in educational publishing, Barron's has helped millions of students reach their academic goals. Our E-Z series of books is designed to help students master a variety of subjects. We are so confident that completing all the review material and exercises in this book will help you, that if your grades don't improve within 30 days, we will give you a full refund.

To qualify for a refund, simply return the book within 90 days of purchase and include your store receipt. Refunds will not include sales tax or postage. Offer available only to U.S. residents. Void where prohibited. Send books to **Barron's Educational Series, Inc., Attn: Customer Service** at the address on this page.

About the Author:

Daniel Mulvey taught high school English for more than thirty-seven years, seventeen in Durham, Connecticut, and more recently at Daniel Hand High School in Madison, Connecticut. He is also the author of Barron's *Write On!*, a grammar and style guide for writers, and numerous articles for *American Heritage*, *On the Water*, and *River & Shore* magazines, and various local newspapers.

SECOND EDITION
© 2009 by Barron's Educational Series, Inc.
© Copyright 2002 by Barron's Educational Series, Inc., under the title *Grammar the Easy Way*.

All rights reserved.
No part of this book may be reproduced or distributed in any form or by any means without the written permission of the copyright owner.

All inquiries should be addressed to:
Barron's Educational Series, Inc.
250 Wireless Boulevard
Hauppauge, New York 11788
www.barronseduc.com

Library of Congress Control No. 2008042424
ISBN-13: 978-0-7641-4261-1
ISBN-10: 0-7641-4261-5

Library of Congress Cataloging-in-Publication Data
Mulvey, Dan.
    [Grammar the easy way]
    E-Z grammar/by Dan Mulvey.—2nd ed.
        p.   cm.
    Includes index.
    Originally published: 1st ed. Grammar the easy way, 2002.
    Summary: Reviews basic grammar, including parts of speech, sentence structure, and subject-verb agreement; provides a manual of usage, instruction on writing paragraphs and research papers, and how to develop one's own style; and includes exercises and a test.
    ISBN-13: 978-0-7641-4261-1
    ISBN-10: 0-7641-4261-5

    1. English language—Grammar.   I. Title.
    PE1112.M85 2009
    428.2—dc22   2008042424

PRINTED IN THE UNITED STATES OF AMERICA
9 8 7 6 5 4 3 2 1

CONTENTS

Preface

This book presents grammar logically and progressively to high school seniors and college freshmen. Starting with the sentence, the book explores facets of grammar, especially the parts of speech, in expanded form. In Chapters 1 to 6 the student will notice that the noun, adjective, and adverb have expanded to include both phrases and clauses. The verb also receives much attention.

After a discussion in Chapter 7 about the types of sentences, the student is directed toward the advanced grammar section, which includes discussions of coordination and subordination, reference of pronouns, agreement of subject-verb and pronoun-antecedent, use of parallel structure, avoiding misplaced and dangling modifiers, and finally a section on sentence variety. The quizzes are cumulative.

Chapter 15 is a manual of usage. The words chosen reflect more than thirty-seven years of corrected papers. From there the book moves right into the writing of paragraphs with several examples from the author and from others more famous.

At the end, style development, mechanics (capitalization and punctuation), and a word or two about spelling complete a logical approach to grammar.

I would like to thank the following for their help and encouragement: Chuck Collins, who started me; Gerry Degenhardt, who still teaches me; my wife, Nancy, who put up with a ton; Gil Cass, who taught me to teach everyone; Art Donaldson, who in seventh and eighth grade taught me grammar for the first time; Dr. Paul Van K. Thompson from Providence College, who insisted we know our grammar.

Sources used for examples of great writing and help with some quizzes:

Page 24 "Blood on the Moon," excerpt from *Abraham Lincoln: The War Years*, Volume IV by Carl Sandburg, copyright 1939 by Harcourt, Inc., renewed 1967 by Carl Sandburg, reprinted by permission of the publisher.

Pages 32–33 excerpt from *Native Son* by Richard Wright, "Flight," HarperCollins Publishers, Inc., p. 45. Copyright 1940 by Richard Wright. Copyright © renewed 1968 by Ellen Wright. Reprinted by permission of HarperCollins Publishers Inc.

Page 39 from "Goodbye to 48th Street" from *The Points of My Compass* by E. B. White. Copyright © 1957 by E. B. White. Originally appeared in *The New Yorker*. Reprinted by permission of HarperCollins Publishers Inc.

Page 57 reprinted with the permission of Simon & Schuster from *The Great Books* by David Denby. Copyright © 1996 by David Denby.

Page 58 from James, Henry, *Henry James, Nine Tales*, "Daisy Miller," Franklin Library, Franklin Center, PA, 1977, pp. 120–121.

Pages 116–117 and 121–122 from Thoreau, Henry David, *A Week on the Concord and Merrimack Rivers*, "Saturday," Parnassus Imprints, Inc., Orleans, MA, 1987, pp. 39–40.

Page 117 from White, E. B., *The Elements of Style*, "An Approach to Style," Macmillan, New York, 1979, p. 82.

Page 120 from O'Brien, Edna, *Down by the River*, "The River," Phoenix Press, Publisher.

Page 120 from Banks, Russell, *The Angel on the Roof,* Stories by Russell Banks, HarperCollins Publishers, Inc., 2000.

Pages 120–121 from Melville, Herman, *Moby Dick*, "The Dart," Easton Press, Norwalk, CT, 1977, p. 307.

Pages 124–125 from Melville, Herman, *Moby Dick*, Easton Press, Norwalk, CT, 1977, p. 13.

Page 129 from Dickinson, Emily, # 1489. Reprinted by permission of the publishers and the Trustees of Amherst College from *The Poems of Emily Dickinson*, Ralph W. Franklin, ed., Cambridge, Mass.: The Belknap Press of Harvard University Press, Copyright © 1998 by the President and Fellows of Harvard College. Copyright © 1951, 1955, 1979 by the President and Fellows of Harvard College.

Page 129 from Whittier, John Greenleaf, "Barbara Frietchie," Memorized by author.

The Sentence

A sentence is a unit of words, complete unto itself, beginning with a capital letter and ending with a period, or question mark, or exclamation mark, and containing a subject, which might not be apparent but certainly is understood, and a predicate, which contains the verb.

There are four types of sentences: simple, complex, compound, and compound-complex. For now, the discussion will concentrate on the simple sentence. Chapter 8 will focus on the complex, compound, and compound-complex sentence.

The eight parts of speech (see Chapter 2), which include the noun (the subject) and the verb, form the building blocks of all sentences, all writing. The "subject" of the sentence may comprise one word (*Jean* bought a present) or many words (*Oak Leaf Marina in Old Saybrook, Connecticut,* launches some of the biggest yachts in New England), as long as those words are connected to the subject. The "predicate" of the sentence comprises the verb (Billy Townsend and Ed Ricciuti *fish)* and any words somehow related to the verb (Bobby Bushnell <u>lost two of his engines on a trip to Montauk with ten of his closest friends</u>). The subject must tell the reader something definitive (in other words, the subject must be a person, place, thing, idea, or quality) (see Chapter 2), and the verb must make the subject do something (with an action verb) or at least exist (with a state of being or linking verb) (see Chapter 5).

There are exceptions to every rule. If, as stated earlier, "the subject must tell the reader something definitive," what is definitive about the subject in the sentences that follow? *It* is possible. *It* will snow tomorrow. *It* galls me that you eat too much. *It* is frustrating to know sometimes what "it" means.

The subject in each case does not mean anything, yet we understand perfectly what the writer (or speaker more probably) intends. Moreover, sometimes the subject does not appear but certainly is understood as in the following: Go. Be quiet! Hand in the papers now. The verbs ("Go," "Be," "Hand") are there but the subject, "you," is not. Clearly though, "you" is understood.

The verb, unlike the subject, has no exceptions. No verb, no sentence. Unless you write like Graham Greene, Edna O'Brien, or Wally Lamb, or if you are writing a grammar book and for emphasis you say "No verb, no sentence," or if you write poetry like Emily Dickinson:

A route of Evanescence with a revolving Wheel.

As a rule, however, high school English teachers and college professors will not allow you to leave out verbs without a hearty chastising, unless you are participating in a creative writing seminar.

Simple Subject, Simple Verb, Complete Subject, Complete Verb

SUBJECT

The subject usually can be narrowed down to a word or name, a noun, that pinpoints what the writer or speaker is highlighting. This one word or name is called the *simple subject*. In the following sentences, notice how the underlined words, the simple subjects, capture the essence of the topic of the sentence:

Leonard Paul Mandak owns and operates a tackle shop in Clinton, Connecticut.
Philip A. Shreffler writes beautiful sea articles.
Projects were completed by Michael Henry McGivern.
Defense brought the Giants to the Super Bowl in 2001 and 2008.

The subject can comprise several words, such as modifiers; these groups of words related to the simple subject make up the complete subject. The complete subjects are underlined, and the simple subjects are in parentheses in the following sentences:

The careful (writer) of prose or poetry must choose words carefully.
(Boats) docked at West Wharf in Madison should be registered with the town hall.
Roxie Strachbein from Orthodontics on the Plateau used to live in Durham, Connecticut.

VERB

Like the subject, the verb may be just one word:

Naomi Jean Siravo owns her own company.
Rose Seward cleans teeth painlessly and thoroughly.
Gail Parent works the computer in the office.

Also, the verb might consist of more than one word:

Kelly Elizabeth Edwards <u>will be having</u> a party for the neighborhood.
Phreadd Nichols <u>can recall</u> baseball trivia better than anyone else.
Wendy Nielsen <u>has been e-mailing</u> her friends for several years.

Also, just as the subject can be one word (simple subject) or comprise many words (complete subject), the verb can be just the verb or the complete verb, sometimes called the predicate. The complete verbs or predicates are underlined in the following sentences (the simple verbs are in parentheses):

Enea Bacci <u>(can charm) an entire room with his beautiful Italian smile.</u>
Bill Vieser <u>(goes) fishing with Peter Weiss, otherwise known as "The Coyote Man."</u>

CONCLUSION

The complete subject and the complete verb (the predicate) make up what is called the simple sentence. In the following simple sentences, the complete subject is underlined while the complete verb, the predicate, is in parentheses:

<u>Jack and Winnie Boudreau</u> (once owned and operated a bagel shop but turned the business over to their children.)
<u>Charlene Ordway of Vermont but formerly of Madison</u> (was voted best looking student eight years in a row.)
<u>Vacationing in Madison, Juliet Nichols</u> (fought a striped bass for three hours and landed the fish herself.)

Note: For a more complete discussion of the subject, see Chapter 2.

TASK 1

In the following simple sentences, place the simple subject in parentheses and underline the complete subject; then, underline the simple verb and place the complete verb, the predicate, in parentheses. (Answers are on page 162.)

1. Roxie Murphy Strachbein, from Orthodontics on the Plateau, used to live in Durham, Connecticut.

2. Ripping a phone book in half, Victor Engel wanted to impress his dramatics class.

3. Gerry Degenhardt, rummaging in the attic, found a photo album filled with pictures of Chuck Collins.

4. Charles Edward Lipnicki, along with Robert Judson "The Stalker" Turton, plays with people's minds incessantly.

5. Dennis Mullin, once a liberal, has turned into one of the biggest conservatives.

Fragment and Run-on

Two of the most common errors in writing and the bane of English teachers worldwide, the fragment and run-on have plagued beginning writers and have caused more graying instructor hair than any other sentence error.

THE FRAGMENT

The *fragment* looks like a sentence because of the capital letter at the beginning and the period at the end, but the fragment is missing either the verb or the subject or both; the fragment sometimes contains an introductory word (like *because*, *although*, *when*, *who*, *whoever*) that subordinates, makes less important grammatically, the thought. A sentence must be a complete thought; complete thoughts are the most important thoughts.

EXAMPLES

At the end of the long day, toiling in the mines.

There is no verb here and therefore no subject. Although "toiling" looks like a verb because of the "-ing," it lacks a helping verb. Also, this group of words begins with a capital letter and ends with a period. It "looks like" a sentence but is not. (See Chapter 3.)

Because Betty Hahn invited my wife and me to her book signing of *Hustled Aboard* at the Agua Restaurant at Cedar Island Marina.

This fragment contains both a subject, "Betty Hahn," and a verb, "invited," but is missing a complete thought. The introductory word "Because," a subordinating conjunction (see Chapter 4), causes this group of words to fall short of a sentence because the thought is incomplete, and therefore less important grammatically than a sentence would be.

CORRECTING FRAGMENTS

Correcting fragments is a simple process. The writer needs to attach the fragment to an existing sentence. Correction of the two preceding examples might look like this:

At the end of a long day, toiling in the mines, <u>Malcolm Stevens MacGruer felt he had made a step closer to amassing a huge fortune</u>. (The underlined part is the sentence to which the fragment is attached.)

<u>We rearranged our schedule</u> because Betty Hahn invited my wife and me to her book signing of *Hustled Aboard* at the Agua Restaurant at Cedar Island Marina. (The underlined part is the sentence to which the fragment is attached.)

THE RUN-ON

Actually a *run-on* sentence is two or more sentences improperly joined by wrong punctuation, no punctuation, or a conjunction that needs help from some kind of punctuation.

EXAMPLES

Dan Dolan tore down his existing house, then he built a new structure known in Madison as the Taj Mahal. (This example, sometimes called a comma fault or comma splice, needs punctuation stronger than a comma to join the two main clauses.)
CORRECTION: Dan Dolan tore down his existing house; then he built a new structure known in Madison as the Taj Mahal.

In interscholastic sports, Connor Dolan ranked in the top ten throughout his high school career he also starred in several musicals, including "Guys and Dolls." (Between "career" and "he" the writer needs some punctuation and/or some connecting word.)
CORRECTION: . . . his high school career, <u>and</u> he also . . .

Diane Dolan jogs along Middle Beach and she hopes that her new house will be ready by fall. (Here the writer needs a comma after "Beach" because "and" is not strong enough to hold the two main clauses together.)
CORRECTION: Diane Dolan jogs along Middle Beach, and she hopes that her new house will be ready by fall.

CORRECTING A RUN-ON SENTENCE FIVE WAYS

Here is a classic, or rather a common, run-on sentence:

Popeye and Pluto often fight over a woman, the winner is not decided until Popeye somehow eats his spinach. (This run-on is actually two independent clauses separated by a comma only—a comma fault or comma splice.)

CORRECTION NO. 1: Make two sentences.

Popeye and Pluto often fight over a woman. The winner is not decided until Popeye somehow eats his spinach.

CORRECTION NO. 2: Join the two clauses by using a comma and a coordination conjunction.

Popeye and Pluto often fight over a woman, but the winner is not decided until Popeye somehow eats his spinach.

CORRECTION NO. 3: Join the two clauses with a semicolon.

Popeye and Pluto often fight over a woman; the winner is not decided until Popeye somehow eats his spinach.

CORRECTION NO. 4: Join the two clauses with a semicolon and a connector with a comma (but not a coordinating conjunction).

Popeye and Pluto often fight over a woman; however, the winner is not decided until Popeye somehow eats his spinach.

CORRECTION NO. 5: Subordinate one of the clauses (see Chapter 8). The author chooses to make one clause, then, less important than the other clause.

Popeye and Pluto often fight over a woman, although the winner is not decided until Popeye somehow eats his spinach.

OR

Even though Popeye and Pluto often fight over a woman, the winner is not decided until Popeye somehow eats his spinach.

The best way to correct this sentence? That question can be answered by the author only.

TASK 2

If the numbered item is a correct sentence, place a "C" next to the number on your paper. If the item is a fragment, place an "F" next to the number; if the item is a run-on, place an "R" next to the number; then rewrite the items marked "F" and "R." With the run-ons, try the five different ways to make corrections. (Answers are on pages 162–163.)

1. Because F. Scott Fitzgerald had to return the publisher's advance for *The Great Gatsby.*

2. Macken Dolan worked out at World Gym with his favorite teacher she tore a muscle and sued his family.

3. Brett Dolan served as the lookout and Matt Gentile rifled the teacher's desk, looking for the answer sheets to tomorrow's quiz.

4. Since Bob Sullivan has served on the Board of Directors for the Madison Country Club.

5. When James Thurber and E. B. White were working for *The New Yorker*, the magazine entertained millions, but when the two left, circulation went down drastically.

6. During the month of May and several days into the month of June.

7. Because Tim Sullivan graduated with honors, he had no trouble landing a job; however, after three months with a prestigious firm, he opted to join the Peace Corps.

8. Frequently goading bartenders to tell the most outrageous jokes about feminism and the Reconstruction of the South.

9. Sandra Beach Barry, strolling down Madison Avenue near 48th Street in Manhattan, near the exclusive store where she used to shop.

10. Joe Peter Votto built a house in Buffalo Bay before he built that house he had lived in Queens.

The Process of Composing a Sentence

Sometimes writing the best sentence possible challenges even the best of writers because all writers are faced with the same types of problems that might look something like this:

1. Will this sentence be a simple, a compound, a complex, or a compound-complex sentence?

2. If the sentence is a simple sentence, will that sentence be long, short, or in between?

3. If the sentence is compound, how will the two (or more) main clauses be connected? Will a transition word be needed? What punctuation will be needed?

4. If the sentence is complex, with what word will the dependent clause be subordinated? Will I use more than one dependent clause?

5. If the sentence is compound-complex, how many dependent clauses will I use? How many independent clauses? What transition words will I need to convey my meaning exactly? What punctuation will I need?

6. I know I should use active verbs, but will a passive verb fit with this sentence I am about to write?

7. Assuming I am writing a paragraph, how obvious do I make the transition from the sentence before and to the sentence following?

8. What words will be appropriate for this sentence?

9. Will the subject come first and then the verb or is there some other way to write this sentence?

10. What type of subordination (or reduction) of thoughts will I use: words, phrases, or clauses?

11. After I write the sentence, is there any thought or word or phrase or clause that needs work?

Writing a sentence, then, is not easy. The process also repeats itself for every sentence written, and then the writer must ask, "Is my paragraph coherent, logical, and most of all, readable. Is my vocabulary appropriate for the subject I have chosen? Is there variety in my sentences? Am I finally developing a style I can call my own?"

How to Become a Better Writer

1. Develop your own vocabulary by reading a variety of authors. Pay attention to their uses of words and never pass over a word that you do not know. Skipping words without getting their meaning is really a reverse form of "word attack": The word attacks the reader instead of the other way around.

2. Keep a journal. Keep it with you and during idle moments write some sentences that are thoughts or direct observations.

3. Write something every day. E-mail, letters, notes, lists (with every item in the same grammatical form), thoughts, and observations. An occasional letter to the editor lets you see your work in print for a more objective view.

4. Learn, once and for all, the rules of grammar.

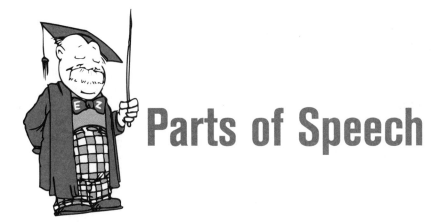

Parts of Speech

Most English grammars start with the parts of speech; consequently, this text does not differ from those grammars. There happens here one slight twist: Rather than consider single words as parts of speech, this section presents phrases and clauses functioning as nouns, adjectives, and adverbs.

Verbs, too, can be presented using more than one word ("should have been elected") as can certain prepositions ("on account of," "because of," and "in spite of") and interjections ("Oh my!"); coordinating conjunctions (and, but, for, or, nor, yet) are single words, but correlative conjunctions (not only . . . but also, whether . . . or, either . . . or, neither . . . nor, both . . . and) are two or more words.

Note: A word, a phrase, or a clause is never a part of speech until it is used in writing or in speech.

Definitions and Characteristics— The Eight Parts of Speech

VERB

See Chapter 5 for a complete discussion of verbs.

- An action word, state of being word, linking word, or a group of words that is the action or link of the subject of the sentence. Some authorities call verbs of two or more words verb phrases, but a phrase is a group of words that has no verb.

Action verb

Using an action verb enables the writer (and the reader) to visualize or feel the process that the subject is going through.

Edward Craig Fritz and Tazo <u>thrashed</u> in the water, but they eventually <u>learned</u> to swim.

"Thrashed" is easy to see; "learned" is not so easy because the "action" is difficult to visualize. However, both are action verbs.

Judy Ann Meade and Brian Joseph Meade <u>promised</u> their teacher that they <u>would behave</u> from now on.

"Promised" can be visualized as well as "would behave," the future behavior.

State of being verb

Clare Quinn <u>is</u> the best pupil in her school, according to her teachers.

In this example, Clare Quinn exists as the best pupil. The sentence speaks of her "state of being."

Linking verb

Sean Banisch <u>remained</u> calm with the pack of dogs barking at him.

"Remained" links "Sean" with "calm."

A "group of words" verb

Matt Banisch <u>has been toiling</u> as a drill instructor for three years.

"Has been toiling" is the indicative progressive, present perfect tense (see Chapter 5).

- Verbs can be active (The subject does the action.) or passive (The subject is acted upon.) (See Chapter 5.)

Active

Casey Speed <u>teaches</u> catechism, <u>runs</u> in the local marathons, and <u>plays</u> the harp at weddings.

Casey does all of those actions.

Passive

Harvey Hall "The Stalker" Thurrott <u>was told</u> to stop laughing in church.

Harvey Hall does not act in this sentence. Someone else told him to stop laughing.

- Verbs must agree with the subject in number (see Chapter 5, the conjugation section).

At Shea Stadium, forty thousand <u>fans boo</u> (both subject and verb are plural)
Aaron Heilman when <u>he is sent</u> (both are singular) in to relieve.
<u>Martha Lovejoy loves</u> (singular subject, singular verb) to travel.

- All sentences must contain a verb (and a subject; see the following section on nouns).

Help me!

The verb is "Help," and the subject "you" is understood. The subject is omitted because the sentence "You help me!" would be awkward.

- All verbs have four principal parts from which all the tenses are formed. The four principal parts: (1) present stem, (2) past tense, (3) past participle, (4) present participle. Some verbs are regular (forming the second and third parts by adding "-ed" or "-d" (look, *looked*, *looked*, looking or brake, *braked*, *braked*, braking), but some principal parts are irregular (cast, cast, cast, casting or bring, brought, brought, bringing). See pages 195–198.

When the third and fourth principal parts are used with *helping verbs*, they become verbs (<u>has been</u> looking, <u>must have been</u> casting, <u>had</u> braked).
When the third and fourth principal parts are used by themselves, with no helping verb, they are either adjectives or nouns (the <u>frightened</u> cat, the <u>madding</u> crowd, <u>burned</u> cookies).

By <u>looking</u> (noun—object of the preposition) cool, Lauri Ann Bartiss landed the job.

<u>Casting</u> (adjective—modifying LHG) the last ballot, Lois Fay Radawich decided the vote for waitress of the year.

(See Chapter 5 for a complete discussion of verbs.)

NOUN

- A *noun* is a word, phrase, or clause that names a person (Mike Attebery), place (Somersetshire), thing (yoyo), idea (rapture), or quality (piety).

Word

Most beginning grammarians think of nouns as words only such as "erne" (a sea bird), "kerry" (a small black dairy cattle of Ireland), "Lhasa apso" (a dog), or "stiver" (a monetary unit of the Netherlands), but students of grammar need to know that groups of words, namely phrases and clauses, have the same status as a word.

Phrase

A group of words without a verb (and therefore no subject).

Magnifying gems (subject, and therefore a noun) prevents jewelry store customers from becoming victims of crime (object of the preposition "from," and therefore a noun).

Before becoming a priest (object of the preposition "before"), Chuck Fador taught industrial arts.

Clause

A group of words with a subject and a verb, but an incomplete thought.

Whoever is responsible for the damage in the auditorium will cause the prom to be canceled unless he comes forward.

"Whoever . . . auditorium" has the same status as "Magnifying gems" and "Chuck Fador"—these sentence elements are all subjects of their sentences: They are all nouns.

- There are several categories of nouns: common, proper, compound, collective, nouns used as adverbs, concrete, abstract, countable and noncountable, and even verbal nouns (gerunds).

Common

Any noun not capitalized: building, prophesy, snob, porch.

Proper

Any noun capitalized because it is specific: Chrysler Building, Coginchaug Regional High School, Kansas, Providence College.

Compound

Any noun made up of two or more words: ice cream, mainstream, textbook, snowmobile, brother-in-law.

Collective

Any noun that in its singular form denotes many within: pod (of whales), herd (of cows), company (of men), army (of ants). *Fowler's Modern English Usage* lists over one hundred collective nouns including this one: "drunkship of cobblers."

Nouns used as adverbs

I went yesterday; Mondays and Fridays Caroline and Danny go to dance lessons; Phyllis and Ed live in West Palm Beach winters but come back to

Madison <u>summers</u> sometimes.

Concrete

Tangible, palpable things(s): rock, basketball, wren, poopbox (for a cat), bungee cord, aroma (like going past a bakery).

Abstract

In the definition of the noun, quality or idea: honesty, ritual, craftiness, piety, development.

Countable

Those nouns that form their plural simply by adding "-s" or "-es" and can be used with an indefinite article: mass (masses), project (projects), course (courses), firm (firms).

Noncountable

Those nouns that have no plural and are not usually used with an indefinite article: adulthood, poverty, peace, magnificence.

Verbal nouns (Gerunds)

These nouns are formed from the fourth principal part of any verb, the present participle. These always end in "–ing": tutoring, reading, throwing, mixing, collecting. The following sentences show the preceding words as subject, direct object, indirect object, object of the preposition, or predicate noun, respectively (See the next section for further explanation of the five functions of the noun):

<u>Hostessing</u> (subject) at Malone's on Sunday makes Jacey Nicole Votto happy.

Keith Hotchkiss loves <u>reading</u> (direct object) Patrick McCabe novels.

Since he was four, Nolan Ryan gave <u>throwing</u> (indirect object) a baseball top priority.

Terri James, by <u>mixing</u> (object of the preposition) certain ingredients, produces the best omelets.

Susan Freytag's favorite hobby is <u>collecting</u> (predicate nominative) stamps of Ireland.

Nouns, regardless of whether they are words, phrases, or clauses, may function as a subject, a direct object, an indirect object, an object of the preposition, or a predicate noun (predicate nominative). To begin the discussion of nouns, we will use words, and save the phrases and clauses for later chapters.

SUBJECT

The *subject* is one of the two main parts of any sentence; only nouns [word(s), phrase(s), clause(s)] can be subjects of sentences. Even the shortest sentence known (Go!) has a subject that is understood, but the imperative here would lose its impact if the person were to include the subject as in "You go!" The subject is what the sentence is talking about; knowing the subject, then, makes the job easier for the reader of a book or for the writer trying to convey an idea.

In the following sentences, the subject is underlined, while the verbs are in parentheses:

In Caron Avery's front yard (is) a <u>statue</u> of a gigantic striped bass.
John Avery's <u>passion</u>, playing the piano, (reveals) his intense fascination with music.
Around the corner from the Woodlawn Roadside Grille (rests) Beth and Michael Vogel's beautiful <u>home</u>.
<u>No one</u> (possesses) more gadgets than does Jack Sanford Davis.
<u>Fred and Susan Parker</u> (lived) near Lexington Avenue.
Bob Schumann's <u>gardens</u> (cause) walkers on Middle Beach Road to stop and stare.

To find the subject:
1. Identify the verb.
2. Ask who? or what? with the verb. The answer will give you the subject of the sentence.

TASK 3

Find the subject of the following sentences using these criteria. (Answers are on page 164.)

1. Frequently parents of small children listen to the wrong authorities of child rearing.

2. After losing three straight games of gin, Costy slammed the cards on the table and left in a huff.

3. Dan Zeoli, during his strenuous workout, pulled a muscle in his lower calf.

4. Classic and Spider Solitaire divert my attention quite often.

5. A full membership discount World Gym offers serious body builders only if full payment accompanies the contract.

6. Government spending on the space program exceeds monies spent on helping the poor.

7. Lobstermen in Connecticut were compensated for their losses in the year 2000.

8. *Fowler's Modern English Usage* and *The Chicago Manual of Style* provide writers invaluable information about language and mechanics.

9. In the back of my mind, there lurks a long-forgotten thought of revenge.

10. While swimming in Lake George, Herb and Gaye Weber suddenly felt something biting their legs.

DIRECT OBJECT

A *direct object* is a noun (word, phrase, or clause) or pronoun that receives action from the subject and verb. Two ideas are implied here: One is that the verb must be a transitive verb and can take an object; the second idea is that a passive verb, linking verb, or state of being verb (be, is, am, are, was, were, and been, which are intransitive) can never "take" an object; the only complements that can follow an intransitive verb are a predicate nominative or predicate adjective.

This does not mean, however, that if there is an action verb, there must be a direct or indirect object. For example:

My horse <u>ran</u> in the Preakness. ("Ran" is an action verb, but there is no direct object.) Unlike the following:

Betty O'Shea <u>ran</u> a (clinic) on how to control husbands. ("Clinic" is the direct object of "ran.")

Following are examples of transitive and intransitive verbs:

Andrew Banisch <u>constructed</u> (transitive verb) a magnificent <u>replica</u> (direct object receiving the action of "constructed") of a World War I biplane.

Shennell Antrobus <u>was honored</u> (intransitive, passive) in high school as a scholar-athlete all over the world. (no complement)

Keith Luckenback <u>looked</u> (intransitive, linking) <u>spectacular</u> (predicate adjective) in *Big River*.

Spike and Pat Burns <u>are</u> (intransitive, state of being) <u>residents</u> (predicate nominative) of Atlanta, Georgia.

Kathryn E. Crockett would have been disappointed (intransitive, passive) had she not landed a job at R. J. Julia's bookstore.

Finding the direct object is easy if you follow this pattern:
1. Locate the verb.
2. Find the subject by asking Who? or What? with the verb.

3. Say the subject first, then the verb and ask Whom? Or What? The answer will give you the direct object.

TASK 4

Go back to the sentences in Task # 3, and now, using the preceding formula, find the direct object. Keep in mind: Every sentence must have a verb and a subject, but every sentence does not contain a direct object. (Answers are on page 164.)

INDIRECT OBJECT

An *indirect object* is a noun, noun phrase, or noun clause or pronoun that receives action from the verb indirectly and answers the questions To whom? For whom? To what? or For what? Like the direct object, an indirect object must have an action verb to function; therefore, a state of being verb or linking verb can never have an indirect object.

EXAMPLE

Cara Banisch gave (action verb) St. Margaret Church (indirect object receiving action indirectly; notice "to" is missing) all her money (direct object receiving the action directly) that she made selling lemonade.

How to find the indirect object:
1. Find the verb.
2. Find the subject.
3. Find the direct object.
4. Ask To whom? For whom? To what? or For what? The answer will be the indirect object.

EXAMPLE

The animal trainer threw the seals a bucket of fish.

Verb—"threw"
Who or what "threw"—animal trainer (subject)
"Animal trainer threw" Whom? or What?—a bucket (direct object)
"Animal trainer threw a bucket" To whom? For whom? To what? For what?—seals (indirect object)

Task 5
Go back to Task # 3 and find the indirect objects. The number of indirect objects you find indicates the frequency with which you will find them (or use them) in the literary world. (Answers are on page 165.)

OBJECT OF THE PREPOSITION

A noun or pronoun that follows a preposition and is linked to another noun or pronoun is called the *object of the preposition*.

EXAMPLES

Bruce Schmottlach wrote the entire score <u>of</u> the school fall musical. ("Of" is the preposition that links "musical," the object of the preposition, with "score.")

Ed and Annette Onofrio announced that they would arrange a party <u>for</u> the entire neighborhood. ("For" is the preposition that links "neighborhood," the object of the preposition, to "party.")

Laurie Nettleton Watson went <u>to</u> school <u>with</u> Bobby Nilson. ("To" is the preposition that links "school," the object of the preposition, to "went." Also, "with" is a preposition linking "Bobby Nilson," the object of the preposition, with "school."

Note: The word "to" is also part of an infinitive: *to* study, *to* turn, *to* forgive. "To," in these examples, is not a preposition.

PREDICATE NOUN (NOMINATIVE)

A *predicate noun* or *predicate nominative* is a word, phrase, or clause that comes after a linking or state of being verb (never after an action verb, however) and that renames the subject:

Cara Banisch was (state of being verb) the <u>reigning Queen of Homecoming</u> (renaming the subject, "Cara Banisch") last fall.

• A sentence must have a subject to be a sentence—the subject of any sentence is always a noun or pronoun. Sometimes, however, the subject is understood to be "you."

(You) Tell me the truth.
(You) Give me a break.
(You) Be quiet!

PRONOUN

- A *pronoun* is a word used in place of a noun. An antecedent is a word or group of words to which a pronoun refers. If the antecedent is singular, the pronoun must be singular. If the antecedent is plural, then the pronoun must be plural (see Chapter 10).

EXAMPLE

Liz Manning told her boss, Tim Joseph Malone, that she was going on vacation.

Both "her" and "she" refer to Liz Manning (the antecedent) clearly (see Chapters 9 and 10).

- All pronouns should have a clear antecedent—in other words, there should be no confusion finding to what or to whom the pronoun refers (see Chapter 10).
- The various types of pronouns are personal (subjective case, objective case, and possessive case), reflexive or intensive, demonstrative, relative, interrogative, extended, and indefinite.

PERSONAL PRONOUNS

Subjective case (used as the subject or predicate nominative)—I, you, he, she, it, we, they

Objective case (used as a direct object, indirect object, or object of the preposition)— me, you, him, her, it, us, them

Possessive case (used to show possession of nouns)—my, mine, your, yours, his, her, hers, its, our, ours, their, theirs.

How many times have you heard something resembling the following statements:

Him and me went to the movies. ("He" and "I" because they are subjects)
Melody Forrest gave no Christmas bonus to Ron and I. ("me" because it is the object of the preposition)

REFLEXIVE OR INTENSIVE PRONOUNS

myself, yourself, himself, herself, itself, oneself, ourselves, yourselves, themselves

"Reflexive" means that the pronoun refers back to the person or thing mentioned:

Wayne Gretsky hurt himself when his stick splintered.

"Intensive" means that the pronoun emphasizes another noun or pronoun:

We finished the project *ourselves* without any help from our neighbors.

These forms should not be used by themselves as a subject, predicate nominative, or an object. But don't mention that rule to the Irish. "Herself is in the other room." or "How's himself this morning?" are as common and understandable as "forty shades of green."

DEMONSTRATIVE PRONOUNS

this, that, these, those

These pronouns "demonstrate" or "point out" certain nouns.

<u>These</u> are my children.
I cannot deal with <u>that</u>.

RELATIVE PRONOUNS

who, whom, which, that, whose

These pronouns introduce an adjective clause and therefore "relate" to the noun (and in rare cases a pronoun).

Dr. Richard E. Kaufman, <u>whose</u> office is at 960 Main Street in Branford, specializes in internal medicine, allergies, and immunology.
I, <u>who</u> think movies intrinsically thin, loved "Castaway" with Tom Hanks.

INTERROGATIVE PRONOUNS

who, whom, whose, which, what
You can almost see the question mark after each of these pronouns.

When Bobby Thomson hit the "shot heard 'round the world" to win the playoff game with the Brooklyn Dodgers, <u>who</u> was on deck?
<u>What</u> Major League player hit a home run his first at bat and then played in more than a thousand games without hitting another one?
(See page 198 for the answers.)

EXTENDED PRONOUNS

whatever (who has not heard this pronoun lately, almost as an interjection—(as in "Whatever!"), whoever, whosoever, whomever

These fit nicely into the beginning of a noun clause:

The race officials will award ribbons to *whoever* finishes the race.

INDEFINITE PRONOUNS

any, anyone, all, each, everybody, everyone, anybody, some, someone, none, no one, both, etc.

These pronouns should be used carefully; otherwise they lead to sweeping generalizations.

Anyone can swim.
Everybody sins.

ADJECTIVE

- An *adjective* is a word, phrase, or clause that modifies (changes, limits, describes, transforms, qualifies) a noun or pronoun: One of the world's influential reference books, *The Oxford English Dictionary*, reigns as the authority of all lexicons. Notice how "world's," "influential," and "reference" cause a dramatic change in "books." "Books," by itself, could mean any book, but with the use of these words, "Books" has been transformed into a particular set of books.

- Adjectives answer the following questions: Which one? What kind? and How many?

  Which one?—Use of the demonstrative pronouns (this, that, these, those) points out: These are the rules you must follow. That is exactly what I mean. Even "the" specifies which one and is the "definite" article.

  What kind?—This is the general category of adjectives: The sleek, sporty, powerful, expensive, noisy, gas-guzzling, fire-engine-red Corvette scared my grandmother. Notice here how "Corvette" is modified or limited or changed into a specific Corvette.

  How many?—Forms of numbers: Fifteen consecutive life sentences Jeffrey Dommers received for his atrocities. Indefinite: Some patience most men need when they hire others.

- Adjectives may be placed before the noun (or pronoun), after the noun (or pronoun), or after a state of being verb or a linking verb.

  Before the noun—This is the usual position of the adjective with its noun: obstreperous child, reticent student, vociferous fan.

After the noun—the waif, <u>tired</u> and <u>hungry</u>; In a good mood, we left the hospital, <u>leaving</u> the children <u>happy</u>. ("Leaving," a participle, modifies "we," while "happy" modifies "children.")

After a state of being or linking verb—My doctor became <u>angry</u> when he found I had gained twenty pounds. Zenobia Frome was <u>aware</u> of her husband's affair. Lenny Wilkens looks <u>fit</u>, just as he did when he played for Providence College.

ADVERB

- An *adverb* is a word, phrase, or clause that modifies (changes, limits, describes, transforms, qualifies) a verb, an adjective, or another adverb.

  Adverb modifying a verb—*Once,* Babe Ruth *playfully* pointed to the spot where he would hit a home run. ("Once" and "playfully" modify the verb "pointed.")

  Adverb modifying an adjective—The *exceedingly* beautiful woman turned everyone's eyes. ("Beautiful" is here just not ordinary "beautiful.")

  Adverb modifying another adverb—The play put on by the high school drama club was <u>very</u> poorly done. ("Very" modifies "poorly," an adverb that modifies "done.")

- Adverbs answer the following questions: How? When? Where? To what extent? (How much? How often?).

- Adverbs of one word almost always come before the word modified, as do those adverb phrases (prepositional and infinitive) except when these phrases introduce the sentence. An adverb clause should be placed as closely as possible to the verb it modifies. I have never found an example of an adverb clause modifying another adverb.

- Adverbs are formed two ways: One is by adding "-ly" to an adjective; sometimes this addition means a change in spelling: holy (adjective), holily (adverb); ready (adjective), readily (adverb); but—mundane (adjective), mundanely (adverb); correct (adjective), correctly (adverb). The other way to form adverbs is to place an adjective in the following formula: in a _____ manner. Placing an adjective in the blank creates an adverb: in a <u>peaceful</u> manner, in a <u>harsh</u> manner, in a <u>boastful</u> manner. The problem with the second approach to forming adverbs is that the writer uses more words than necessary, just like this explanation.

- "Only" as an adverb is misplaced probably more than any other word.

TASK 6

Choose and label the adjectives and adverbs in the following sentences. (Answers are on page 165.)

1. Carefully, Lynnea Bidwell put one foot on the thin ice to test its safety.

2. Sam and Matthew Mulvey, running in the house, smashed some valuable crystal accidentally.

3. Many fishermen definitely think that beautiful Long Island Sound is theirs only.

4. Marvelous Marvin Murphy instantly recognized the hidden shoal and steered safely to the east.

5. Trixi and Jett, two of the neighborhood dogs, behaved strangely because they had devoured a five pound bag of Tootsie Rolls.

6. Savannah Sinon stubbornly doubted the bartender when he told her that he was writing a grammar book.

7. Black seabass might be the best tasting fish ever eaten.

8. Mixing business with pleasure, Bob Sullivan extensively toured Vienna and neighboring towns.

9. Dale Lewis Mullin wants to play for the New York Mets.

10. Decorous and quiet, Kippy Martin moderately chastised her daughter's teacher.

PREPOSITION

- A *preposition* is a word that links a noun or a pronoun *with* some other word (usually a noun or a verb) or words in the sentence. Never heard that definition before? Look at the definition again. The preposition "*with*" links "some other word" with "a noun or a pronoun."

- A preposition almost always precedes the noun or pronoun linked. Perhaps this condition prompts scholars to say that a writer should never end a sentence with a preposition. (See Appendix 2 for a list of prepositions.) However, sometimes a preposition does end the sentence as in the following: In desperate situations, what should a person resort <u>to</u>?

In the following sentences, the two words linked are underlined and the preposition is in italics:

Thomas Pare, (<u>director</u> *of* <u>Post Road Physical Therapy</u>), schedules his patients hourly. ("of" joins "director" and "Post Road Physical Therapy.")

Cathy Bacci found out that (<u>many</u> *of* her <u>relatives</u>) (<u>came</u> *from* <u>Ireland</u>.) ("of" joins "many" and "relatives"; also, "from" joins "came" with "Ireland.)

(*At* the <u>Surf Club</u>, Jane Broadbar Lee <u>loves</u>) (<u>to frolic</u> *in* the <u>sand</u>.) ("At" joins "Surf Club" with "loves," and "in" joins "to frolic" with "sand.")

Kathleen Blair Leisure throws (<u>parties</u> *in* her <u>backyard</u>). ("In" joins "parties" and "backyard.")

CONJUNCTION

- A *conjunction* is a word or words used to join other words, phrases, or clauses.

  Joining words—apples <u>and</u> pears, amphibians <u>or</u> reptiles,

  Joining phrases—on the top <u>and</u> on the bottom, hitting the books <u>and</u> sleeping eight hours

- Coordinating conjunctions (and, but, or, nor, yet, for) and correlative conjunctions (either . . . or, neither . . . nor, not only . . . but also, both . . . and, whether . . . or) join two or more words with words, phrases with phrases, and clauses with clauses. (See Chapter 11.)

- Never is a word joined with a phrase or a phrase with a clause. (See also Chapter 11.) Using coordinating conjunctions usually requires a comma before the conjunction when used to construct a compound sentence. (See Chapter 7.)

- Adverbial conjunctions (although, if, because, since) join subordinate clauses with main clauses. (See Chapter 4.)

- In most cases, conjunctions appear between other words, but on rare occasions, a conjunction can introduce a sentence or a paragraph. For example, "and" introduces epics to show that there was a connection between the story that follows and past incidents, implying that although this story is immense, there was a series of incidents preceding.

INTERJECTION

- An *interjection* is a word or group of words expressing emotion or feeling, however slight. Also, this part of speech doesn't fit into any of the other categories of the parts of speech.

Well, I do not think so.

To describe the accident, all the witness could say was "ugh."

Marvelous! Marvelous! I shall relate the incident to my aunt!

TASK 7

In the following paragraph by Carl Sandburg concerning the death of Abraham Lincoln, parts of speech are underlined. You are to identify them. (Answers are on pages 166–167.)

The (1) moment of high fate was (2) not seen (3) by the theater audience. (4) Only (5) lone man saw (6) that moment. (7) He was the Outsider. He was the one (8) who had (9) waited and (10) lurked and (11) made his (12) preparations, planning and plotting that he (13) should be the single and lone spectator of what happened. He had come (14) through the outer door into the hallway, fastened the (15) strong though slender bar into the (16) two-inch niche in the brick wall, (17) and braced it against the (18) door panel. He had moved (19) softly to the (20) box door and through the little hole he (21) had gimleted that afternoon he had studied the box occupants and his Human Target seated in an (22) upholstered rocking armchair. Softly he had opened the door and stepped (23) toward his prey, in his right hand a (24) one-shot brass derringer pistol, a little (25) eight-ounce vest-pocket weapon (26) winged for death, in his left hand a steel dagger. (27) He was cool and precise and timed his (28) every move. He raised the derringer, (29) lengthened his right arm, ran his eye along the barrel in a line with the head of his victim less than five feet (30) away—and pulled the trigger.

TASK 8

Try your skill at using all the parts of speech in as few words as possible. (See page 167 for a possible answer.)

Can the same word be used as every part of speech? Man?

1. Presiding at the bench, the <u>man</u> in the robe was Peter Keeton Leisure. (noun, used as the subject)
2. The <u>man</u> hater subjected herself to criticism from her colleagues. (adjective, modifying "hater")
3. <u>Man,</u> I did it! (interjection, expressing emotion)
4. I <u>manned</u> the oars in true sailor fashion. (verb, past tense of "to man")
5. The dancer, <u>man</u>-handled by the aggressive patron, fled to the dressing room. (If "handled" is an adjective, then "man" here is an adverb.)
6. There is no way "man" can be a pronoun, preposition, or a conjunction. Or is there?

The parts of speech learned well will aid you in learning phrases, the next logical step on the grammar ladder. With phrases, however, you need to concentrate on nouns, adjectives, and adverbs, the only ways phrases are used and identified in grammar, with the possible exception of verbs, as in "verb phrases."

Phrases

The next step in learning grammar, the phrase, benefits the student in both writing and reading: In writing, the ability to use phrases effectively allows for a greater range of ideas, those ideas that cannot be stated in single words. In reading, learning phrases enables the student, with one eye movement, to read larger sentence units rather than read word by word. (See Appendix 4 for further explanation.)

Phrase

A group of words without a subject and verb, used as a part of speech. Presented here are prepositional phrases, gerund phrases, participial phrases, appositive phrases, and infinitive phrases.

Prepositional Phrases

Prepositional phrases are either adjectives or adverbs depending upon how they are used. A prepositional phrase begins with a preposition (See the complete list of prepositions in Appendix 2) and ends with a noun or pronoun.

At Coginchaug Regional High School, Carol Luckenback taught English. (prepositional phrase modifying "taught," the verb, and therefore functioning as an adverb because adverbs modify verbs)

The gym at Coginchaug Regional High School is sold out when the girls or the boys play basketball against their league rivals. (same phrase functioning as an adjective modifying "gym," a noun)

Wally Camp, for thirty years the director of athletics at Coginchaug, set victory records in soccer and in basketball. (adjective phrases modifying nouns)

In 1892, James J. Corbett became the undisputed heavyweight champion of boxing. (First prepositional phrase is an adverb; the second is an adjective.)

SAME PHRASE USED TWO DIFFERENT WAYS

Ann Leyshon Fink found <u>in her drink</u> a borer bee. (adverb phrase because it modifies the verb "found")

The bee <u>in her drink</u> made Ann Fink fraught. (adjective phrase because it modifies the noun "bee") Challenge: Say quickly the last three words of the sentence five times.

Conclusion: A prepositional phrase is not an adjective or adverb until used in a sentence.

<u>From the shore</u>, Tim Malone caught fifteen striped bass. ("From the shore" modifies the verb "caught" and therefore is an adverb.)

Gregory Mulvey visited his friend <u>from the shore</u> of the Mediterranean. ("From the shore" modifies "friend," a noun, and now functions as an adjective.)

Task 9

In the following sentences, pick out the prepositional phrases and decide whether they are adjective or adverb. (Answers are on pages 167–168.)

1. On his way to the gym, Geoff Knowlton witnessed a UPS truck collide with a motorcycle.

2. Behind the elm tree near the movie theater, Gerard Bernard McGuiness discovered a purse in the shape of an ear.

3. In spite of his efforts to win the lottery, Gerry Knowlton continued to lose on the scratch-off tickets.

4. Throughout her college career, Marcat Knowlton dazzled her professors with her outstanding achievements.

5. Until recently, Leslie Donkin worked as an analyst in London, England.

6. Without a moment's hesitation, Lauren Blumen pulled up stakes, married Cobi, and now teaches English at a university in Israel.

7. Most teachers go beyond their limits to help students help themselves.

8. During the exhibition at the local high school, certain recalcitrants scattered litter all over the parking lot.

9. Given proper instruction, learning-disabled youngsters often succeed where nonaffected youngsters fail.

10. Upon hearing the tale of woe, the priest suggested that the teen confessing to him seek help from the youth officer.

Participial Phrases

Participial phrases function as adjectives and contain a present or past participle. Participles all tend to end in "-ing" (present participles), "-ed," "-d," "-en," "-n," or "-t" with a few exceptions like "swum" and "hung" (past participles); participial phrases are made up of a participle along with an object or modifier or both. These adjective phrases are usually placed as near as possible to the word(s) they modify. Participles are the third and fourth principal parts of verbs. (See Chapter 5.)

Fortified against a surprise attack, Macbeth's dwindling army had almost deserted their leader. (participial [with a past participle] phrase with "against a surprise attack," a modifier)

Singing "Aida" in the shower, Gary Dobrindt aggravated his neighbors. (Present participle with a direct object ["Aida"] and "in the shower" modifying "Singing.")

Marching in the St. Patrick's Day Parade, Celsus Long showed his pride in Ireland. ("Marching" is the participle, "in the . . . Parade" is an adverb modifying "Marching," and the entire phrase modifies "Celsus Long.")

Dedicated to the spiritual development of the less fortunate, Mother Theresa denied herself to help others. ("Dedicated" is the participle; "to the . . . fortunate," the modifiers; and the entire phrase modifies "Mother Theresa.")

The obstreperous students snickered as the substitute teacher, bent out of shape, threatened to report them to the principal. ("Bent" is the participle and "out of shape," the modifier.)

Thrashing the shore with magnificent force, the Nor'easter pounded the rocky coast of Maine. ("Thrashing" is the participle here with "shore" its direct object and "with . . . force" the modifier.)

Gerund Phrases

Like any noun, the gerund functions as a subject, direct object, indirect object, object of the preposition, or predicate nominative. The *gerund phrase* is made up of the present participle ("-ing") and can contain an object and/or a modifier (and sometimes many modifiers). The gerund is a verbal noun.

GERUND PHRASE AS A SUBJECT

Making the varsity in any Division I school in any sport discourages those without scholarships. ("Making" is the subject of the sentence, "varsity" is its direct object, and "in any . . . sport" are the two modifiers.)

Selling boats demands product knowledge. ("Selling" is the subject of "demands," and "boats" is the object of "Selling.")

GERUND PHRASE AS A DIRECT OBJECT

My father once considered swimming the English Channel but decided against the plan. ("Swimming" is the direct object of the verb "considered," while "the English Channel" is the direct object of "swimming"; there are no modifiers in this phrase except "the.")

Note: Here is a case where a direct object has its own direct object, but do not forget that "swimming" is formed from the verb "swim."

The rookie catchers practiced protecting the plate. ("Protecting" is the object of "practiced," and "plate" is the object of "protecting.")

GERUND PHRASE AS AN INDIRECT OBJECT

If high school students give learning grammar a fair chance, their writing will improve immensely. ("Learning" is the indirect object of "give" and "grammar" is the direct object of "learning," the gerund.)

Note: See how the word "to" is left out of the sentence, thus creating the indirect object.

My brother Mark Mulvey once gave swinging a golf club his undivided attention. ("Swinging" is the indirect object with "to" omitted. "Attention" is the direct object, and "club" is the object of "swinging." "A," "golf," "his," and "undivided" are modifiers.)

GERUND PHRASE AS AN OBJECT OF THE PREPOSITION

Local authorities once tried to control the feline population by spaying the female cats that inhabited the alley between the post office and the theater. ("Spaying" is a gerund, the object of the preposition "by" and "the female cats" is the object of "spaying.")

Courtney Clinton pleased her English teacher by memorizing completely twelve of Emily Dickinson's most difficult poems. ("Memorizing" is the object of the preposition "by"; "completely" modifies "memorizing" and "twelve" is the object of memorizing.)

GERUND PHRASE AS A PREDICATE NOMINATIVE

Ron Caturano's hobby was <u>collecting exotic bottles</u> for his homemade sambuca. (The verb is "was," not "was collecting"; "collecting" is a gerund used as the predicate nominative renaming "hobby," while "exotic bottles" serves as the direct object of "collecting." This phrase contains both an object and a modifier.)

Rob Gourley's great accomplishment is <u>singing "Rocky Raccoon."</u> ("Singing" renames "accomplishment" and therefore is the predicate nominative. The song title is the object of "singing.")

Missy Knowlton's forte in field hockey was <u>slashing from the left side</u>. ("Slashing" is the predicate nominative renaming "forte," and "from the left side" is a modifier.)

CONCLUSION

Gerund phrases, which contain a present participle and/or a complement and/or a modifier, function as nouns.

AS THE SUBJECT: <u>Selling boats</u> demands product knowledge.

AS THE DIRECT OBJECT: The rookie catchers practiced <u>protecting the plate</u>.

AS THE INDIRECT OBJECT: My brother once gave <u>swinging a golf club</u> his undivided attention.

AS THE OBJECT OF THE PREPOSITION: Courtney Clinton pleased her English teacher by <u>memorizing completely twelve of Emily Dickinson's poems</u>.

AS THE PREDICATE NOMINATIVE: Missy Knowlton's forte in field hockey was <u>slashing in from the left side</u>.

Appositives and Appositive Phrases

An *appositive* is always a noun. Usually (see below) an appositive follows immediately after a noun, is sometimes set off by commas, and renames or emphasizes the noun it follows. Remember that an appositive does not contain verbs.

Barron's, <u>a publisher of books ranging from grammar texts to collections of kittens</u>, boasts of the finest employees in the world.

Notice that the appositive has one word renaming the noun it follows—"publisher" renames "Barron's"—and that the entire phrase adds to the definition of "Barron's."

My brother <u>Mark</u> lives in Reignier, France and works in Geneva, Switzerland. One word "name" appositives usually do not need commas, but there is a caution here: If there are more of the group, more brothers or sisters, for example, then no commas are needed. No commas means restrictive; *restrictive* means that if you take that element out of the sentence, the sentence changes its meaning. The element is essential, necessary, and therefore no commas. Putting commas around an appositive tells the readers that this part of the sentence is not needed, but it does add to the information of the sentence.

The Littoral Society, <u>an organization for the preservation of the striped bass,</u> offers tagging kits for local anglers who want to participate in the program. Taking the appositive out of the sentence does not change the meaning of the sentence.

Herman Melville's novel <u>*Oomo*</u> is based on his experiences living with cannibals. (Placing commas around *Oomo* would indicate it's the only novel Melville wrote.)

Steve Zielinski, <u>Mother Nature's gift to World Gym,</u> eats puffed rice for breakfast. (Sometimes appositives reveal the tone of the writer.)

The appositive, the noun or noun phrase that explains or adds information to the noun that follows, for the sake of variety might appear *before* the noun:

<u>The owner of the Schooner Wharf Galley in Key West,</u> Britt Evalena Henriksson Worthington, won a dance contest sponsored by the Gunnar Johnson School of Dance.

<u>The most outstanding teacher in the North Haven area,</u> Peg Robertson, once traveled around the world three times in one year.

Infinitive Phrases

Infinitive phrases can be used as three parts of speech: noun, adjective, or adverb.

NOUN: <u>To teach youngsters grammar</u> becomes a daunting task for beginning educators. (This phrase functions as the subject of "becomes"; the phrase contains two objects, one direct ["grammar"] and one indirect ["youngsters"].)

ADJECTIVE: The old textbooks <u>to be thrown away</u> were bundled by the custodian. ("to be thrown away" modifies "textbooks," and "away" is the phrase's modifier.)

ADVERB: Joe Gallagher always goes to great lengths <u>to make his customers feel at home.</u> (This phrase modifies the verb "goes" and is therefore an adverb, while "customers" is the object. Also, there is a second infinitive phrase "feel at home," but the "to" is missing—but implied.)

Task 10

The following sentences contain all the different types of phrases. Next to the number of the sentence, list the phrases, and identify them. (Answers are on page 168.)

1. Navigating through Plum Gut, Bobby Bushnell expertly steered *Dynamite* around the Tea Pot, heading for Lake Montauk.

2. Gary, the man with the reputation as the top salesman for Bayliners and other brands, set a record by selling fourteen motoryachts in a six-month period.

3. To help me in my new sales career, Marshall Corona gave me a book that told all the secrets of selling.

4. After a grueling day at the Norwalk Boat Show, the sales crew was treated to a grand supper at MacDonald's.

5. Not watching what he was doing, Dwight Palmer fell down the last six steps of the staircase and broke his big toe.

Task 11

The following paragraph contains examples of various phrases. Next to the number on your paper, identify the phrases and their uses according to the following directions. (Answers are on page 169.)

    A. Prepositional phrase (Adjective or adverb?)
    B. Participle (What word does it modify?)
    C. Participial phrase (What word does it modify?)
    D. Gerund (What function of the noun is it?)
    E. Gerund phrase (What function of the noun is it?)
    F. Infinitive (Noun, adjective, or adverb?)
    G. Infinitive phrase (Noun, adjective, or adverb?)
    H. Appositive (What function of the noun is it?)
    I. Appositive phrase (What function of the noun is it?)

    He tried (1) <u>to move his hands</u> and found that they were shackled (2) <u>by strong bands</u> of cold steel to white wrists of policemen (3) <u>sitting to either side of him</u>. He looked round; a policeman stood (4) <u>in front of him</u> and one in back. He heard a sharp, metallic click and his hands were free. There was a (5) rising murmur of voices and he sensed that it was caused by his movements. Then his eyes became (6) <u>riveted on a white face,</u> (7) <u>tilted slightly upward</u>. The skin had a quality of taut anxiety and around the oval (8) <u>of white face</u> was a framework of whiter hair. It was Mrs. Dalton, (9) <u>sitting quietly,</u> her frail, waxen hands folded in her lap. Bigger remembered as he looked at her that moment (10) <u>of stark horror</u> when he had stood at the side of the bed in the dark blue room (11) <u>hearing his heart pound against his ribs</u>. With his fingers upon the pillow (12) <u>pressing down upon Mary's face</u> (13) <u>to keep her from mumbling</u>.

(from Native Son by Richard Wright)

Task 12

Follow the instructions to compose well-thought-out sentences. (Suggested answers are on pages 169–170.)

1. With prepositional phrases as adverbs and as adjectives;

2. With participial phrases: at least two, with one at the beginning;

3. With gerund phrases as a subject, direct object, indirect object, object of the preposition, predicate nominative;

4. With infinitive phrases as a noun, adjective, or adverb.

Note: These units can be, for each number, in one sentence or in individual sentences.
Additional note: Gerunds, participles, and infinitives can function outside of phrases. Use of these words by themselves sometimes stresses ideas, sometimes belittles ideas.

You judge:

- *To be* or not *to be* . . .
- *To err* is human . . .
- *Dancing* I can't.
- *Running*, I tripped.
- *Concentrating* bothers me.
- *Declaiming* makes me nervous.
- My uncle is *arresting*.

Words. Phrases. Next are clauses. Again, in studying clauses, you will concentrate on nouns, adjectives, and adverbs, just like in the study of phrases.

Clauses

In a logical developmental study of language, clauses in the pecking order rate the third step (not in importance but in a gradual unfolding of the grammatical truth) among words, phrases, clauses, sentences, paragraphs, essays, short stories, book-length-fiction, and book-length nonfiction. Careful writers introduce clauses into their writing for variety, emphasis, and added information; perceptive readers recognize larger thought units with longer eye span, with faster reading, and with greater understanding of the text.

Clauses are either independent, meaning they can stand by themselves and make sense (in other words *sentences*), or dependent, meaning they cannot stand by themselves, and to make sense, they need to attach themselves to other words (usually sentences). *Independent clause*, *main clause*, and *sentence* are synonymous and the terms may be used interchangeably. Also, *dependent* and *subordinate* are synonymous and used interchangeably. *Subordinate* also implies that the thought expressed by the *subordinate clause* is an important fact, but less important than the sentence itself; the subordinate clause is a part of a sentence that may be omitted or included, depending upon the whim of the writer. If the subordinate clause may be omitted without changing the meaning of the sentence, this clause is called *nonrestrictive* or *nonessential*. If the clause cannot be removed without changing the meaning of the sentence, then this clause is called *restrictive* or *essential*.

Sentences and Clauses

SENTENCE: Michelle Riccio works as a secretary at Cedar Island Marina. (Stands by itself because it makes sense, has a subject and a verb; it is a sentence; it is independent.)

DEPENDENT CLAUSE: When Kevin Simmons hit a monster home run against the Guilford Indians. (Looks like a sentence, but it does not make sense. It needs to attach itself to a sentence to make sense. It looks like a sentence, also, because it contains a subject and verb. Also, the response of the reader to that dependent clause is "Well, yes, what happened next?")

When Kevin Simmons hit a monster home run against the Guilford Indians, he broke the game wide open. (Now the dependent clause makes sense because it is attached to a sentence. Also, the sentence is flimsy because of the pronoun "he," but it makes sense with the addition of the clause.)

Note: If the sentence is called the main clause, then the dependent clause is called the subordinate clause. By using these two elements, the writer stresses thoughts when he uses main clauses and relegates other thoughts less important when he uses dependent clauses.

Note the following:

(Although the Yankees played several games with replacements), the team hung together and eventually won the pennant.

The writer stresses the cohesiveness of the team and the winning of the pennant by placing those ideas in the main clause (also, independent clause). The clause is underlined. The subordinate clause (in parentheses) is dependent on that main clause; the dependent clause cannot stand by itself.

Another example:

Bill and Betty Holliday, (who have lived in several parts of the world), love Madison, Connecticut, the best. (The adjective clause in parentheses could not possibly stand by itself, even as a question.)

DEPENDENT CLAUSE

A *dependent clause* is a group of words with a subject and verb: noun clauses, adjective clauses, and adverb clauses function in the same manner as words and phrases, except clauses tend to be longer units. These units look like sentences because they contain a verb and a subject; however, they also contain an introductory word, sometimes implied, which shows some relationship to another word; therefore, these clauses cannot stand by themselves. They need to attach themselves to make sense.

NOUN CLAUSE

A *noun clause* is a group of words that function as a subject, direct object, indirect object (in rare cases), object of the preposition, or predicate nominative.

SUBJECT: Whoever is responsible for the graffiti on the north side of the high school building should turn himself in to the police. ("Should turn" is the verb; who or what should turn? "Whoever . . . building" is the answer and therefore the subject of the sentence.

Note: Look at the underlined words: "is" is the verb and "whoever" is the subject of the clause.

DIRECT OBJECT: Gene Calzetta clicks away with the remote and chooses whatever suits his fancy. (The clause is the direct object of "chooses"; "whatever" is the subject, "suits" is the verb, and "his fancy" is the direct object of "suits.")

INDIRECT OBJECT: Chuck Collins assigned whoever had an "A" a project dealing with forensics. ("Project" is the direct object while "whoever had an 'A' " is missing "to" in front of it and therefore qualifies as an indirect object; of course, "whoever" is the subject of the clause while "had" is the verb of the clause.)

OBJECT OF THE PREPOSITION: Terri James would present the Culinary Arts Award to whoever baked the cake with the most chocolate. ("Whoever" is the subject of the clause; also, notice how the clause is placed next to the preposition "to.")

PREDICATE NOMINATIVE: The Culinary Arts Award was whatever struck the fancy of the presenter. (Here "whatever . . . presenter" renames the "Award" and follows a verb of being; therefore, we have a predicate nominative clause with a subject "whatever" and a verb "struck.")

ADJECTIVE CLAUSE

An *adjective clause* is a group of words with a subject and verb and introductory relative pronoun (who, whom, which, that); this group of words modifies a single noun or pronoun.

Butch Cooney, who tells some of the wildest jokes, travels extensively throughout Europe. (Notice how the introductory word "who" is also the subject of the clause.)

After reading from his text on Shakespeare, Harold Bloom entertained questions that the audience enthusiastically asked about Macbeth. (Notice the word "that" is immediately next to "questions," the word to which it relates. The writer must always place the adjective clause next to the noun or pronoun it modifies to avoid misplacement.)

The program that captures the imagination of a huge audience usually receives the most awards at the end of the year. (Notice the lack of commas: This is a restrictive clause; it belongs in the sentence and is essential to the meaning. Without it, the sentence would read "The program usually receives the most awards at the end of the year." It doesn't make sense, does it?)

The Woodlawn, which was owned by the proprietor of The Dolly Madison Inne, had a long history in the town of Madison, Connecticut. (Removing the clause does not change the meaning of the sentence; therefore, this clause is nonessential.)

Task 13

Decide which of the adjective clauses in the following sentences need commas (nonrestrictive or nonessential) or do not need commas (restrictive or essential). Rewrite the sentences that need, or do not need, commas. Place a "C" next to the numbers of the sentences that are correct. (Answers are on page 170.)

1. Russell Banks who wrote such works as *Affliction* and *Continental Drift* has recently published a collection of short stories called *Angel on the Roof.*

2. Lenny Wilkens who coached in the NBA has won more games as a coach in the NBA than any other coach.

3. The book, that I consider the best teaching tool for vocabulary and reading comprehension, is *Ethan Frome* by Edith Wharton.

4. The three tenors, who sang in the competition last Friday, won second place.

5. The seniors, who applied to colleges early this year, were all accepted.

6. Anjelica Riccio who ranked in the top ten at her school delivered an address to the parents on Back-to-School Night.

7. The strange looking man, whom I met on the elevator, turned out to be my third cousin.

8. The baseball program which was dropped at Providence College to make room for women's sports probably will never be activated until more males enroll.

9. Joe Martirano, who majored in English at Providence College, owns property in Massachusetts, in New York, and in Florida.

10. The student, who ranked as the most likeable child at St. John's School, was Caroline Fitzgerald who also had fourteen "A's" on her report card.

ADVERB CLAUSE

An *adverb clause* is a group of words with a subject and a verb and an introductory adverb that designates when, where, how, and to what extent and expresses reason. Adverb clauses usually modify verbs but, like single adverbs, also modify adjectives; however, one has to ponder long and hard before he can think of an adverb clause modifying another adverb. Usually, when an adverb clause comes at the beginning of a sentence, it is set off by a comma:

When Alyssa Stone called the other day, she told us that she landed a job at Kiwi John's on Nantucket.

When the adverb clause is in the middle of the sentence, it usually is set off by a comma, but at the end of the sentence it is set off by a comma only if the thought in the clause is abruptly negative to the words before.

Joan Venditto, the former principal of Our Lady of Mercy School, travels to Nantucket every year, although she never goes fishing. (comma needed because the thought is contrary to the preceding thought—signaled by "although")

But: Joan also visits New Bedford before she lands on Nantucket. (no comma needed)

When Bill Reilly visited Key West, he caught from the dock near his condominium several large fish. (adverb clause modifying the verb "caught" and set off by a comma because it comes first in the sentence)

Joe Pegnataro creates beautiful landscape, even though he never took lessons. (adverb clause modifying the verb "creates" and the comma is used because of the contradicting thought)

Note: It is virtually impossible to misplace an adverb clause that modifies the verb.

As calm as Dave Nelson seems when approaching a ball in a sand trap, internally butterflies play havoc with his psyche. (adverb clauses, one modifying "calm," the other modifying the verb "seems")

Task 14

The following sentences contain the three types of dependent clauses. Identify the clauses and state their function or what they modify. (Answers are on pages 170–171.)

1. Whatever Lola wants, Lola gets.

2. Before he enlisted in the Marines, Bill Reilly hunted wild boar in Australia.

3. In 1937, my parents, who were delighted with their offspring, decided that I would become a schoolteacher.

4. Whenever Elizabeth Ann McGuinness and John James McGuinness go on a long bus trip, they each take several books which help them with their ennui.

5. Dale Lewis Mullin gave presents to whoever praised his schoolwork.

6. Daniel Francis Xavier Mulvey, who was the sports editor of the *New Haven Register* and who gave Albie Booth the nickname of "Little Boy Blue," could spell any word in the English language.

7. Whatever bid Gerd Nelson makes while playing bridge usually pleases her partner.

8. While he was vacationing in Florida, Tony Barone caught fifty-eight grouper which he sold to local fish stores.

9. After the World Trade Center buildings fell, the American way of life that we had known changed forever.

10. On September 11, otherwise known as 9/11 or 911, most Americans remember where they were at the time of the tragedy.

REVIEWING CHAPTERS 3 AND 4

Task 15

This paragraph is from an essay by E. B. White. Read it carefully and then answer the questions that follow. (Answers are on page 171.)

For some weeks now I have been engaged in dispersing the contents of this apartment, trying to persuade hundreds of inanimate objects to scatter and leave me alone. It is not a simple matter. I am impressed by the reluctance of one's worldly goods to go out again into the world. During September I kept hoping that some morning, as if by magic, all books, pictures, records, chairs, beds, curtains, lamps, china, glass, utensils, keepsakes would drain away from around my feet, like the outgoing tide, leaving me standing silent on a bare beach. But this did not happen. My wife and I diligently sorted and discarded things from day to day, and packed other objects for the movers, but a six-room apartment holds as much paraphernalia as an aircraft carrier. You can whittle away at it, but to empty the place completely takes real ingenuity and great staying power. On one of the mornings of disposal, a man from a second-hand bookstore visited us, bought several hundred books, and told us of the death of his brother, the word "cancer" exploding in the living room like a bomb detonated by his grief. Even after he had departed with his heavy load, there seemed to be almost as many books as before, and twice as much sorrow.

In the preceding paragraph, identify the following:

1. The first prepositional phrase you read.

2. The first gerund phrase.

3. The first participial phrase.

4. The first infinitive phrase.

5. The first noun clause (which contains a participial phrase and four prepositional phrases).

6. The first adverb clause.

7. Two more infinitive phrases.

8. Two more participial phrases.

Task 16

Try writing sentences according to the directions that follow. (Answers are on pages 171–172.)

1. Beginning with a prepositional phrase.

2. Beginning with two or more prepositional phrases.

3. Beginning with a direct object.

4. Beginning with a participial phrase.

5. Beginning with a gerund phrase used as the subject.

6. Beginning with an infinitive phrase.

7. Beginning with an adverb clause.

8. Beginning with a noun clause used as the subject.

9. With an adjective clause that needs commas—in other words, is nonessential or nonrestrictive.

10. With an adjective clause that needs no commas—in other words, is essential or restrictive.

The Verb

Tense

Tense means "time," time shown by the verb. Of course, there is the past (Using only 20-pound test line, my nephew Doug once <u>caught</u> a 175-pound Yellowfin tuna.), the present (My other nephew Quippy <u>runs</u> a clam boat out of Milford Landing in Milford, Connecticut.), and the future (Ronnie <u>will</u> never <u>forgive</u> me for casting better than he did at the fishing show.) come to mind immediately, but the past perfect (Young Ethan Frome <u>had had</u> many opportunities to become a scientist, but he chose to marry his cousin Zenobia and wallow in poverty.), the present perfect (I <u>have attended</u> Long Wharf Theater for fourteen years.), and the future perfect (Bill Clinton, 59, <u>will have written</u> four books by the time he reaches 70.) provide writers with every "time" situation they need. Let's look more closely at the underlined verbs:

- *caught*—Simple past tense. The action is completed, over, done with, and the verb "caught" implies Doug might not catch another Yellowfin in a similar situation.

- *runs*—Present tense and more. This verb implies habitual action, action that occurs over a period of time, and tells the reader that Quippy not only has done this job for a while but also will continue until he resigns.

- *will* (never) *forgive*—Future tense indicates later time but also implies a continuance, an extension (especially with the *adverb* "never").

- *had had*—Past perfect shows a completed action just as the simple past does; however, the past perfect also places this completed action *before* some other past action that occurred later. Both are completed actions: one happened before the other. (See also "Sequence of Tenses" in this chapter.)

- *have attended*—Present perfect shows a completed action begun in the past extending to the present time. The writer implies that she has gone to the plays at Long Wharf for fourteen years and that she will continue to attend.

- *will have written*—Future perfect, showing action that has not taken place, can also be expressed by the simple future (Bill Clinton will write . . .); consequently, many writers eschew the future perfect.

HOW TENSES ARE USED

PRESENT TENSE

The *present tense* is used to show time in various ways: action happening now, action that happens as a regular occurrence, action that is historical, and action in the future.

Action happening now

Bill Woods <u>is traveling</u> (action happening at the present time) to Cranston to have dinner at the Twin Oaks. Sonia Pugh personally <u>trains</u> aging men who are on their way out. (Notice here the ongoing action.)

Action as a regular occurrence (also called habitual action)

Steve and Mimi Adkins <u>visit</u> (and notice here how future action is implied because they probably will go again) Ireland every six months on business (action happening regularly).

Historical present

Babe Ruth <u>strides</u> to the plate, <u>glares</u> at the pitcher, and <u>points</u> to the place in right centerfield where he will hit the next pitch for a home run. (The verbs "stride," "glares," and "points" indicate present time that had already taken place, but the writer wishes to bring the reader into the past and constructs the action as if it is occurring now.)

Present tense indicating the future

The present tense is often used to indicate what might happen later.

The weatherman said it <u>is going</u> to rain for the next two weeks. ("Is going" is present progressive (see discussion later), but there is no doubt about the future rain.

Gwen Goodman <u>is attending</u> law school starting next September. (The action has not yet taken place, but there is no doubt about the future indication.)

PAST TENSE

The *past tense* indicates a completed action, a simple action that is over and done with.

My Uncle George <u>fought</u> in World War II.
Julie Christina Votto and Jeannie Ann Votto <u>rooted</u> for the Giants in 2007.
George Fischer <u>ran</u> The Madison Beach Club for thirty-five years.

Use of the past implies that perhaps the action will not occur again.

FUTURE TENSE

Future tense indicates (by using "shall" or "will") that the action has not happened yet but some time later it will (or is intended). The old rule to show the simple future said: Use "shall" with "I" and "we"; use "will" with "you," "he," "she," "it," or "they." If a subject's determination to accomplish something is to be implied, however, the rule is reversed with "will" used with "I" and "we," but "shall" with "you," "he," "she," "it," and "they."

Note: Slowly, but definitely, the distinction between *shall* and *will* are fading fast. This author is in agreement with R. W. Burchfield that the careful writer will consult *Oxford English Dictionary* when the question of using *shall* or *will* arises.

The Ladies Club of Madison <u>will fete</u> Nadia Fischer for causing her husband's success.
Barbie and Matt Albert <u>will start</u> a college fund for their new daughters.
I <u>shall bake</u> a blackfish pie for you when you come to dinner.

PRESENT PERFECT TENSE

The *present perfect tense* indicates an action that is completed in the past but extends to the present time. Time that is continuous or sporadic but that happens many times (or at least twice) is implied.

Because of his intense desire to catch a trophy smallmouth bass, Richard Landino <u>has fished</u> Squam Lake for the last twenty years.
Joe Guglielmo <u>has opened</u> still another store, this one specializing in fireplaces.
You <u>have missed</u> your chance to go to the concert.

PAST PERFECT TENSE

The *past perfect tense* indicates completed time in the past that has taken place before some other indicated past and completed time.

My mother complained that I <u>had</u> not <u>cleaned</u> my room. (The "not cleaning of the room" took place before "mother complained.")
Before he consulted a doctor, Andrew Zingone <u>had experienced</u> loss of memory with numbers for several years. (The "experiencing loss" took place before the "consulting.")

Authors sometimes use the past perfect to guide the reader into a *flashback*, a literary device to recall past events even though the story is now in the present. Once in the past, the past perfect may be abandoned for the simple past tense.

FUTURE PERFECT TENSE

Future perfect tense indicates a time in the future completed before some other completed time in the future.

Missy Frey <u>will have matriculated</u> at twelve universities by the year 2018. (Right now, in 2009, she has matriculated in only two, but she plans to further her education.)

By Memorial Day, Chipper Williams <u>will have entertained</u> several thousand picnickers.

Note: The future perfect is almost non-existent because many writers believe that the simple future expresses what the future perfect expresses, with no change in meaning. Look at the two sentences above with the simple future substituted for the future perfect:

Missy Frey <u>will matriculate</u> at twelve universities by the year 2018.
On Memorial Day, Chipper Williams <u>will entertain</u> several thousand picnickers.

HOW TENSES ARE FORMED

Every verb in English is composed of four principal (main) parts: the first, the present stem (from which the present and the future are formed); the second, the past tense; the third, the past participle (from which the perfect tenses are formed); and the last, the present participle (from which the progressive mood is formed). Years ago, students memorized the irregular verbs, irregular in the sense that they defy rules, unlike regular verbs, which form the past and the past participle simply by adding "-ed," or "d": "look" becomes "looked," and "brake" becomes "braked"; the irregular verb "cast," which is the same in the present stem, past tense, and past participle, must be memorized because there is no rule governing its spelling. If you are not sure about what form of the verb to use, dictionaries tell you if the verbs are regular (adding "-ed" or "-d") or irregular (cast, cast, cast, casting). By the way, all verbs are set in the particular order of present stem, past tense, past participle, and present participle. Here are a few, but check Appendix 3 for a more complete list, and you can also see how a dictionary helps.

Present Stem	Past Tense	Past Participle	Present Participle
bring	brought	brought	bringing
sing	sang	sung	singing
dive	dived (or dove)	dived (or dove)	diving
run	ran	run	running
inter	interred	interred	interring
hunker	hunkered	hunkered	hunkering
hang	hung (a picture)	hung	hanging
hang	hanged (a person)	hanged	hanging

Voice

ACTIVE VOICE

In the *active voice*, the subject of the sentence performs the action. The strength of these verbs forces the action of the sentence forward. These verbs enable the reader to visualize what the subject is doing.

Milk <u>curdles</u>.
Susan E. Kelley <u>taught</u> reading for thirty years.
Trailer trucks <u>roared</u> past me.
Brian and Ann Kelley <u>have resided</u> in Long Beach, California, for several years.

PASSIVE VOICE

In the *passive voice*, the subject of the sentence is acted upon. When a verb is used in the passive voice, the subject no longer acts but rather has something done to it. In the following examples, notice how the passive voice is easily changed to the active voice.

PASSIVE: *Angela's Ashes* <u>was written</u> by Frank McCourt.
ACTIVE: Frank McCourt <u>wrote</u> *Angela's Ashes*.
PASSIVE: Marianne Hughes McGuinness <u>was warned</u> by her sister not to tell the joke about the English teacher.
ACTIVE: Janice Kelley Yeager's sister <u>warned</u> her not to tell the joke about the English teacher.
PASSIVE: The case of the missing teenager <u>was indagated</u> thoroughly, but no conclusion <u>was reached</u>.
ACTIVE: Police <u>indagated</u> thoroughly the case of the missing teenager but <u>reached</u> no conclusions.

This concept of passivity, then, poses its own problems. In my thirty-seven years of teaching English, most of the first few high school essays turned in to me contained huge numbers of passive verbs. I returned the papers with notes in the margin asking that the verbs be changed to active voice. I would add that a paper three to ten pages long needs no passive voice. Now, as I reread the first sentence of this paragraph, I would change the definition of passive voice to: "The subject of the sentence does nothing when the verb is passive."

That is not to say the passive voice cannot be used. For example, if the subject of a sentence is somewhat indefinite, or if what happened to the subject is more important than the subject itself, then the passive voice might be used. Perhaps the best advice is: Use the passive voice sparingly.

PASSIVE: The murderer was hated by the victim's family. (The subject, "the murderer" is a no-name subject. "Victim's family" is no less definite. Is the active better here?)

ACTIVE: The victim's family hated the murderer.

Task 17

The following sentences contain the passive voice; your job is to rewrite them in the active voice. For example,

PASSIVE: After the prom was postponed, the students were advised that the event would be rescheduled.

ACTIVE: After the principal <u>postponed</u> the prom, he <u>advised</u> the students that he <u>would reschedule</u> the event.

(Answers are on page 172.)

1. The young man in the blue suit had been seen at the afternoon movies often.

2. Until now, fishermen were instructed to pick up after themselves, especially at West Wharf.

3. If you have permission to drive your parents' car, you should be taught the rules of the road.

4. My cat was taken to the vet's with a golf-ball sized tick bite.

5. Teachers were told that the school year would be extended for two months with no summer vacation.

6. Conductors on Metro North were given an extra bonus even though extra trains were disconnected.

7. The heat in the house was turned on to the highest degree setting, but the old house with the dilapidated shutters remained cold.

8. In 2000, Alex Rodriguez was signed to the biggest amount ever received, at that point, by a Major League player.

9. The wait staff at the Malone's are instructed to consider the customer first.

10. The computer was given to me by my students.

Mood

INDICATIVE MOOD

The verb indicates (points out, denotes, states, specifies, manifests) what the subject is doing (active) or what is being done to the subject (passive) in the indicative mood.

EXAMPLE

ACTIVE: Ron demonstrated his casting ability. (In the perfect tenses, notice how the third principal part is used.)

PASSIVE: Bobby's boat was washed by the crew at The Boat Center. (Notice that in the passive indicative, the third principal part is used in every tense.)

INDICATIVE PROGRESSIVE MOOD

In the *indicative progressive mood*, the verb indicates what the subject is doing over a period of time: Jessica and Jimmy are making several renovations to their new house. (Progressive indicative is always active—never passive.)

EMPHATIC MOOD

The verb emphasizes or stresses the action in the *emphatic mood*. It uses the present stem and the past tense of "do": Matthew did try to catch a fish but went home after he fell into the water. ("Did" puts emphasis on the verb "try." This mood uses only the present and the past—none of the perfect tenses.)

SUBJUNCTIVE MOOD

Like the emphatic mood, the *subjunctive* is used for a particular purpose and in the present tense and past tense only. In the present, we use the infinitive of the verb without the "to" in the three persons, singular and plural. In the past, we use the verb "were." The subjunctive is used as follows:

- *To express a wish*: I (wish, desire, desiderate, ache) that the Mets be champions in the next World Series.

- *To express a condition contrary to fact*: If the football were kicked just a little to the left, the Hand Tigers might be champions today.

- *To command*: Our chemistry teacher, Mr. Shermer, (commanded, ordered, demanded, requested, bade, gave orders) that we hand in our homework on time.

- *To express a condition*: (On condition that, Provided that, Supposing that) the train does not arrive, we probably should take a cab.

- *To express a suggestion*: Tom Rylander, the mayor of Madison, (suggested, mentioned, submitted, propounded) that the irate citizen quiet down.

- *To express a hypothesis*: The lawyer (postulated, guessed, theorized) that his client be involved in the scheme to kidnap Ralph Garcia.

State of Being and Linking Verbs

STATE OF BEING VERBS

Writers should use the following state of being verbs sparingly as main verbs: be, is, am, are, was, were, been. *State of being verbs* are verbs that make a statement of existence. These verbs can be used by themselves as the main verb and do not necessarily need a complement or completer.

I am.
She is.

Both these statements, showing simple existence, can stand alone with full meaning. Also, these verbs may be followed by an adjective (a predicate adjective) or a noun (a predicate noun).

We are <u>hungry</u>. (predicate adjective describing the subject "We")

LINKING VERBS

Use of the following linking verbs (underlined) should be considered carefully because these verbs, like state of being verbs, merely join the subject of the sentence with an adjective, noun, or pronoun (in parentheses): <u>appear</u> (strange), <u>seem</u> (dubious), <u>stay</u> (sweet), <u>remain</u> (angry), <u>look</u> (fine), <u>smell</u> (rancid), <u>taste</u> (funny), <u>become</u> (senile), <u>grow</u> (cold), <u>turn</u> (rusty), <u>sound</u> (squeaky), <u>get</u> (mad), <u>feel</u> (headachy), <u>go</u> (ballistic). Since these verbs are also used as action verbs, you can use a test to tell whether the verb is action or linking. Substitute a corresponding form of the verb "seem" for the verb in question. If the sentence makes sense, the verb is linking. If the sentence doesn't make sense by the substitution, the verb is active.

EXAMPLES

Pete <u>appeared</u> listless after pulling thirty of his lobster traps. ("Seemed" makes sense when substituted for "appeared." Therefore, "appeared" is linking.)

Pete <u>appeared</u> at the Happy Hour at his usual time. ("Seemed" does not make sense in this sentence; therefore, "appeared" in this sentence is active.)

The milk <u>smelled</u> rancid. ("Seemed" makes sense here too. Therefore "smelled" is a linking verb.)

I <u>smelled</u> smoke. ("Seemed" does not work here. "Smelled," therefore, is an active verb.)

Task 18

In the following sentences, determine whether the verbs underlined are linking verbs or active verbs. (Answers are on page 173.)

1. As the Chocolate Lab <u>smelled</u> the garbage can, his owner noticed a distinct vapor emitting from underneath the lid.

2. Margaret Mary McGuinness <u>looked</u> stunning in her new sequined ball gown.

3. After delivering the baked goods to the Madison Coffee Shop, Elizabeth Ann Meriano <u>remained</u> for a cup of coffee.

4. When faced with disaster, Michael Henry McGivern <u>became</u> a different person.

5. Elisabeth Anne McGuire sent the dessert back because when she <u>tasted</u> it, her eyes watered.

6. Ernest Shaw <u>felt</u> wonderful after a refreshing nap.

7. Corinne Therese Moriarty <u>appeared</u> with her friend at the opening of the opera season in Milan.

8. With the bases loaded and no outs, the pitcher <u>stayed</u> calm enough to strike out the side.

9. The inside of the cabin <u>grew</u> dismal as the sun disappeared.

10. David James Klein, the new superintendent of the Madison, Connecticut, school system, <u>brought</u> a breath of fresh air to the formerly stale office.

Conjugation

To conjugate a verb is to present a schematic of the inflectional forms. In other words, a *conjugation* points out the changes that occur within tenses and between tenses. What follows is the conjugation of the verb "to see," an irregular verb that has four parts, all different.

Indicative Mood, Active Voice: see, saw, seen, seeing

Person	Singular	Plural
Present		
First person	I see	we see
Second person	you see	you see
Third person	she, he, it sees	they see
Past		
First person	I saw	we saw
Second person	you saw	you saw
Third person	she, he, it saw	they saw
Future		
First person	I will see	we will see
Second person	you will see	you will see
Third person	she, he, it will see	they will see
Present Perfect		
First person	I have seen	we have seen
Second person	you have seen	you have seen
Third person	she, he, it has seen	they have seen
Past Perfect		
First person	I had seen	we had seen
Second person	you had seen	you had seen
Third person	she, he, it had seen	they had seen
Future Perfect		
First person	I will have seen	we will have seen
Second person	you will have seen	you will have seen
Third person	she, he, it will have seen	they will have seen

Indicative Mood, Passive Voice: see, saw, seen, seeing

Person	Singular	Plural
Present		
First person	I am seen	we are seen
Second person	you are seen	you are seen
Third person	she, he, it is seen	they are seen

	Past	
First person	I was seen	we were seen
Second person	you were·seen	you were seen
Third person	she, he, it was seen	they were seen

	Future	
First person	I will be seen	we will be seen
Second person	you will be seen	you will be seen
Third person	she, he, it will be seen	they will be seen

	Present Perfect	
First person	I have been seen	we have been seen
Second person	you have been seen	you have been seen
Third person	she, he, it, has been seen	they have been seen

	Past Perfect	
First person	I had been seen	we had been seen
Second person	you had been seen	you had been seen
Third person	she, he, it had been seen	they had been seen

	Future Perfect	
First person	I will have been seen	we will have been seen
Second person	you will have been seen	you will have been seen
Third person	she, he, it will have been seen	they will have been seen

Indicative Progressive Mood, Always Active Voice: see, saw, seen, seeing

Person	Singular	Plural
	Present	
First person	I am seeing	we are seeing
Second person	you are seeing	you are seeing
Third person	she, he, it is seeing	they are seeing
	Past	
First person	I was seeing	we were seeing
Second person	you were seeing	you were seeing
Third person	she, he, it was seeing	they were seeing
	Future	
First person	I will be seeing	we will be seeing
Second person	you will be seeing	you will be seeing
Third person	she, he, it will be seeing	they will be seeing
	Present Perfect	
First person	I have been seeing	we have been seeing
Second person	you have been seeing	you have been seeing
Third person	she, he, it has been seeing	they have been seeing

	Past Perfect	
First person	I had been seeing	we had been seeing
Second person	you had been seeing	you had been seeing
Third person	she, he, it had been seeing	they had been seeing

	Future Perfect	
First person	I will have been seeing	we will have been seeing
Second person	You will have been seeing	you will have been seeing
Third person	she, he, it will have been seeing	they will have been seeing

Emphatic Mood, Always Active Voice (present and past only): see, saw, seen, seeing

Person	Singular	Plural
	Present	
First person	I do see	we do see
Second person	you do see	you do see
Third person	she, he, it does see	they do see

	Past	
First person	I did see	we did see
Second person	You did see	you did see
Third person	She, he, it did see	they did see

Subjunctive Mood, Always Active Voice (present, using the present stem throughout: see, saw, seen, seeing and past, using "were" only without any principal part of any other verb)

Person	Singular	Plural
	Present	
First person	I see	we see
Second person	you see	you see
Third person	she, he, it see	they see

	Past	
First person	I were	we were
Second person	you were	you were
Third person	she, he, it were	they were

Sequence of Tenses

QUESTION: What tense should follow what tense?

ANSWER: Sometimes the use of one tense after another depends on the situation created by the writer. First, as writers proceed with a sentence, they should be careful to use the same tense in direct statements:

Harry Winchell <u>popped</u> the cork on the champagne, <u>proposed</u> a magnificent toast, and then <u>treated</u> his guests to a magnificent feast. (All verbs are in the past tense; see also Chapter 11.) Bobbi Winchell *cooks* wonderful meals, *tells* incredible jokes, and *looks* like a movie star all the time. (All the verbs are in the present tense; see also Chapter 11.)

Second, when one of the four present tenses (present, present perfect, present progressive, present perfect progressive) is the verb in the main or independent clause, the verb in the subordinate or dependent clause can be present tense, past tense, or future tense.

Present (in main clause) with present, past, and future (in the dependent clause)

Karen Gebauer Craig <u>does</u> (present) crosswords in pen

because she <u>is</u> (present) extremely bright.

Erin Marie Connelly <u>waits</u> (present) on tables in a restaurant because her father <u>insisted</u> (past) that she earn some money.

Because her mother <u>will be</u> (future) a principal in Madison for another five years, Kim Cristina <u>studies</u> (present) at Central Connecticut, near her home.

Present perfect (in main clause) with present, past, and future (in the dependent clause)

Paul L'Amoureaux <u>has studied</u> (present perfect) antiques for over forty years because he <u>likes</u> (present) old things.

Kenny Endline Taylor's daughter *has graduated* (present perfect) from Harvard before her brother <u>became</u> (past) a physician.

Fred and Joanne Grube <u>have purchased</u> (present perfect) an old house in North Guilford because they <u>will retire</u> (future) soon.

Present progressive (in main clause) with present, past, and future (in the dependent clause)

While she <u>waits</u> (present) in the Dolly Lounge for her mother to batch out, Haley Lynn Albert <u>is entertaining</u> (present progressive) with several Irish songs.

Erin Mulvey and Mary Alice Cooper <u>are cooperating</u> (present progressive) with local officials after the mayor <u>caught</u> (past) the two raiding the town garage refrigerator.

Dennis Chan is vacationing (present progressive) in Detroit although he will move (future) on to Chicago before the first of the month.

Present perfect progressive (in main clause) with present, past, and future (in the dependent clause)

Shelly-Ann Latoya Allen Jones has been watching (present perfect progressive) Eddie Murphy movies because she likes (present) the way he speaks.

Suzy Ashman, the beautiful princess, has been practicing (present perfect progressive) on the lute for three years, although she never read (past) music in her life.

Lance and Julie Abbott have been paying (present perfect progressive) rent for several years, although soon they will move (future) into their new house.

Third, with some of the past tenses (past, past perfect, past progressive, and past perfect progressive) in the main or independent clause, the verb in the dependent clause should logically complement the verb in the dependent clause.

Past (in the independent clause)

Bill Boyd told (past) the Shellfish Commission that the local clammers had violated (past perfect) several regulations during the past year. The past perfect is needed (in the dependent clause) because it indicates a time (that is, the violation had already taken place) in the past that occurred before another time (the telling of the Commission—this action took place *after* the violations).

Past perfect in the independent clause

Hank Puciato had argued (past perfect) about politics before the first selectman quieted (past) him with sound small-town politics. (The "arguing" took place before the "quieting.")

Past progressive in the independent clause

Art Schneider was donating (past progressive) millions to the Blackstone Library because he had thought (past perfect) that rewards would happen. (He thought first about the rewards, then donated—both actions occurring in the past.)

Past perfect progressive in the independent clause

The ferris wheel had been whirling (past perfect progressive) out of control until one of the carnival employees threw (past) the emergency switch. (The "whirling" took place before the "throwing" of the switch.)

Fourth, the future tense in the independent clause can take the present, past, or present perfect tense.

Future (in the independent clause) with the present tense (in the dependent clause)

Nancy Mulvey <u>will be jumping</u> (future) for joy when she <u>finishes</u> (present) the painting. (Shows that both actions will occur at the same time.)

Future (in the independent clause) with the past (in the dependent clause)

Chip Johnson <u>will</u> definitely <u>make</u> (future) himself a bundle if he <u>invested</u> (past) wisely. (This construction shows an earlier action at the same time of the future.)

Future (in the independent clause) with the present perfect (in the dependent clause)

Providence College basketball <u>will suffer</u> (future) if the recruiting program <u>has</u> not <u>improved</u>. (This construction shows future action earlier than the action of the independent clause.)

Fifth, with the future perfect in the independent clause, use the present or present perfect tense in the dependent clause.

Future perfect (in the independent clause) with the present

Danny Fitzgerald <u>will have set</u> (future perfect) a record for the number of jelly donuts he <u>eats</u> (present).

OR

Danny Fitzgerald <u>will have set</u> (future perfect) a record for the number of jelly donuts he <u>has eaten</u> (present perfect).

Notice how in both cases, the meaning does not change.

Sixth, use the present infinitive to show action that happens at the same time of the verb or action later than the verb.

Present infinitive showing same-time action as the verb

Gerry Degenhardt <u>roots</u> (present) for the Yankees <u>to win</u> (present infinitive) the pennant.

Present infinitive showing action after the time shown by the verb

Bill Dowling <u>would have liked to promote</u> his RockCats better, but the Twins, the parent club, held him back. ("To promote," the infinitive, is expressing the same time as the verb, "would have liked.")

Seventh, use the perfect infinitive to show action that takes place earlier than the time of the verb: Larry Ciotti <u>would love to have seen</u> some of the running backs at Yale make the All-Ivy Team. ("Would love," the verb designating the present, and "to have seen," the perfect infinitive, designate prior time.)

Task 19

Some of the following sentences are written correctly, but in some the verbs need changing. Change any passive verb (or state of being verb) as the main verb to an active verb. Place a C next to the correct sentences; rewrite the incorrect ones. (Answers are on page 173.)

1. Maggie Ruth Maddox greeted customers at the Olive Garden in Milford, Connecticut, bakes the absolute best apple pies, and was recognized as Model Citizen of the year in her hometown.

2. Alyssa Stone was playing the violin when one of the strings snapped and injured Larry, her strange cat.

3. Josh Stone was kept after school because he pulled the pigtails of the girl sitting in front of him.

4. At Our Island Home on Nantucket, Lisa Haye arranges the work schedules for the nurses, was selected as Nurse of the Year, and won the Bake-Off Contest sponsored by the Women's Club.

5. If Larry Webb was a little more intense, he might have landed that huge bass off Madeket.

6. The principal surmised that the young lad standing in front of him is the one who pulled the fire alarm.

7. I think that I make the right move last Thursday.

8. Barack Obama is considered to be one of the top politicians, but he was thought to be too young to be president; he will prove critics wrong.

9. Macbeth believed that if he stays within the walls of his castle he could outlast the onslaught of Malcolm and Macduff.

10. Playing Spider Solitaire is addicting, running is good for one's health, and donating to charities fulfilled my soul.

6

Review of Chapters 1-5

In the following paragraph (from *Great Books* by David Denby), there are items underlined. At the end of the paragraph, follow the directions. (Answers are on page 174.)

Now, <u>for the first time</u> (1), my mother's <u>dropping out of school at fourteen</u> (2) hurt her badly. She had few interests <u>to draw on or cultivate</u> (3), and she was too proud, after years of achievement, <u>to accept instruction</u> (4). She lacked the patience <u>to read fiction</u> (5) and the information and curiosity to read, say, history, so she read biographies of actresses, duchesses, and gigolos and went to the movies <u>a great deal</u> (6). For once, I could help, but there were never enough movies or the right ones, and the complaints arrived like a <u>pelting</u> (7) rainstorm <u>on my head</u> (8). Tradesmen and dentists cheated her; everyone lied. She was suddenly <u>helpless</u> (9), she <u>who had been a master of trade</u> (10). For years, I had been <u>wary</u> (11) of her—I had loved <u>her</u> (12), but I had been wary—and now she wanted <u>everything done for her</u> (13). She wanted to be taken care of, yet she wouldn't accept <u>care</u> (14). She would never consider <u>visiting a shrink</u> (15), and the sole meeting <u>I was able to arrange with a psychiatric social worker</u> (16) turned <u>into a comic disaster</u> (17). Like mighty Oedipus, she would shatter any mirror <u>that you held up to her</u> (18). And so, <u>unseen</u> (19) and <u>unseeing</u> (20), she was <u>relentless</u> (21) in her woe, and these were days <u>when I shut my heart against her</u> (22).

Identify the underlined parts with the following:

    A. Adjective clause
    B. Adverb clause
    C. Direct object
    D. Gerund phrase
    E. Infinitive phrase

F. Noun phrase used as an adverb
G. Participle
H. Participial phrase
I. Predicate adjective
J. Prepositional phrase
K. Adjective

The following paragraph from *Daisy Miller* by Henry James has items underlined. Identify the underlined parts according to the directions after the paragraph. (Answers are on pages 174–176.)

The young girl and her cicerone were (1) <u>on their way</u> (2) <u>to the Gate</u> (3) <u>of the enclosure</u>, (4) <u>so that Winterbourne</u>, (5) <u>who had but lately entered</u>, (4) <u>presently took leave of them</u>. A (6) <u>week</u> afterwards he went (7) <u>to dine at a beautiful villa on the Caelian Hill</u>, and, on (8) <u>arriving</u> dismissed his (9) <u>hired</u> vehicle. The evening (10) <u>was charming</u>, and he promised (11) <u>himself</u> the (12) <u>satisfaction</u> of (13) <u>walking home beneath the Arch of Constantine and past the vaguely-lighted monuments of the Forum</u>. There was a (14) <u>waning</u> moon in the sky, and her radiance was not (15) <u>brilliant</u>, but she was veiled in a thin cloud-curtain (16) <u>which seemed to diffuse and equalize it</u>. (17) <u>When, on his return from the villa (it was eleven o'clock), Winterbourne approached the dusky circle of the Colosseum</u>, it occurred to him, (18) <u>as a lover of the picturesque</u>, (19) <u>that the interior, in the pale moonshine, would be well worth a glance</u>. He turned aside and walked to one of the empty arches, near which, (20) <u>as he observed</u>, an open carriage—(21) <u>one of the little Roman street-cabs</u>—was stationed. Then he passed in, (22) <u>among the cavernous shadows</u> of the great structure, and emerged (23) <u>upon the clear and silent arena</u>. The place had never seemed to him (24) <u>more</u> (25) <u>impressive</u>. (26) <u>One-half</u> of the gigantic circus was in deep shade, the other was sleeping in the luminous dusk. (27) <u>As he stood there</u> he began (28) <u>to murmur Byron's famous lines, out of "Manfred"</u>; but (29) <u>before he had finished his quotation</u> he remembered (30) <u>that</u> (31) <u>if nocturnal meditations in the Colosseum are recommended by the poets</u>, (30) <u>they are deprecated by the doctors</u>. The historic atmosphere was there, (32) <u>certainly</u>; but the historic atmosphere, (33) <u>scientifically considered</u>, was no (34) <u>better</u> than a villainous miasma. Winterbourne walked to the middle of the arena, to take a more general (35) <u>glance</u>, (36) <u>intending thereafter to make a hasty retreat</u>. The great cross in the center was covered with shadow; it was only as he drew near it (37) <u>that he made it out distinctly</u>. Then he saw (38) <u>that two persons were stationed upon the low steps</u> (39) <u>which formed its base</u>. One of these was a woman, (40) <u>seated</u>; her companion was standing in front of her.

Number your paper from 1 to 40. Identify the sentence elements in the paragraph from *Daisy Miller*. Use the following to identify:

A. Prepositional phrase (adjective or adverb?)
B. Gerund
C. Gerund phrase
D. Participle
E. Participial phrase
F. Appositive
G. Appositive phrase
H. Adjective clause
I. Noun or pronoun (subject, direct object, indirect object, predicate noun)—specify the function
J. Adverb clause
K. Predicate adjective
L. Noun used as an adverb
M. Infinitive
N. Infinitive phrase
O. Noun clause
P. Adverb (word)
Q. Verb phrase
R. Sentence

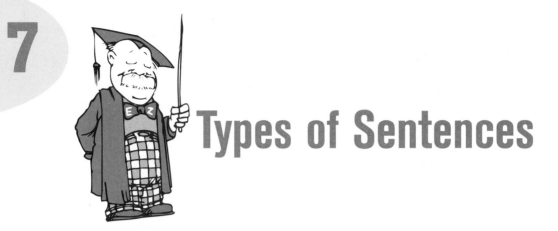

Types of Sentences

The four types of sentences—simple, compound, complex and compound-complex—sometimes cause nightmares for students, on occasions baffle the teacher on how to teach the types, but for centuries have provided writers with essential tools that prevent tedious writing. Sentences may be written or spoken as a statement (Ellen Breen bartends for private parties.); sentences may be spoken or written as a question (How many home runs did Babe Ruth hit in World Series competition? See Appendix 1, page 176 for the answer); sentences may be spoken or written as a command (Put your books on the floor and stop talking immediately.); finally, sentences may be spoken or written as an exclamation, usually accompanied by the exclamation mark (!). (I have just won a million dollars!)

Simple Sentence

A *simple sentence* is a sentence with one subject (which can be multiple or compound) and one verb (which also can be multiple or compound).

The shortest simple sentence? Go. It has a verb, the only word showing, and a subject, you, that is understood.

Basic simple sentence

Thomas Wolfe wrote *The Web and the Rock* in 1937. (one subject, "Thomas Wolfe," and one verb "wrote")

Simple sentence with a compound subject

Thomas Wolfe, Herman Melville, Emily Dickinson, and Robert Frost take up much of my reading time. (four subjects, the four authors, and one verb, "take")

Simple sentence with a compound verb

Peter Newcombe sailed his boat to Nantucket, chaired various projects for the Exchange Club, and ran an insurance firm on the side. (one subject, "Pete Newcombe," and three verbs, "sailed," "chaired," and "ran")

Simple sentence with a compound subject and compound verb

Ron Freytag, Peter Boswell, Bruce Keeton, and Gene Calzetta drove to Fairfax, Virginia, participated in a charity golf tournament, won first prize, and got lost on the way home. (four subjects and four verbs)

Compound Sentence

A *compound sentence* is two or more separate sentences (or main clauses) joined properly with punctuation.

Compound sentence with two main clauses

The Hand Tigers Women's Softball Team ran up a string of eleven victories, but in the crucial last game of the season they lost to Coginchaug 4–3. (Two sentences, closely related, joined by a comma and a conjunction (See Chapter 2, "Conjunctions.") Notice also that there are no other clauses, other than the two main clauses.)

Compound sentence with three main clauses

For extracurricular work, Joe Tenszar drove the bus for the women's basketball team, Bill Ostrander helped the custodians after school, and Jen Degenhardt coached the Women's Track Team. (three sentences, closely related, joined by commas and a conjunction)

Note: in *Fowler's Modern English Usage*, Revised Edition, R. W. Burchfield states that a compound sentence is one with a compound subject or verb. Modern grammarians would disagree.

Complex Sentence

A *complex sentence* contains one sentence (or main clause) with one or more dependent clauses (see Chapter 4).

Complex sentence with one dependent clause (in italics)

Jack Duggan, The Wild Colonial Boy, lost his life in the Australian Outback *because he had shot James McAvoy*. (Notice how the dependent clause cannot stand alone here, but depends on the sentence for its existence.

Complex sentence with two dependent clauses (in italics) ***and one main clause***

Anne Mulvey, *who grew up in Paris,* drives quickly from one place to another *since her time is precious.* Notice the commas around the adjective clause because the clause is nonessential; also notice that there is no comma separating the adverb clause at the end of the sentence. But in the following:

Before Joe Louis went into the army, he was Heavyweight Champion of the World. The adverb clause at the beginning of the sentence is set off by a comma. Many grammarians say this rule is hard and fast; others say a comma is not needed if the clause is short or if there is no confusion by leaving it out.

Complex sentence with three dependent (adverb, adjective, and noun) clauses (in italics)

Whenever Richard Cory went down town, the citizens, *who were gathered in the square,* stared at him thinking *he was a strange duck.* Notice the word "that" is left out of the noun clause and the appropriate commas are inserted around the other two clauses.

QUESTION: How many dependent clauses can a complex sentence have? As many as the writer chooses, as long as they make sense.

Compound-Complex Sentence

A *compound-complex sentence* contains two or more sentences (main clauses) with one (or more) dependent clauses.

Compound-complex sentence, basic variety (with main clauses underlined and the dependent clause in italics)

If I could live my life over, <u>I would try to play Major League Baseball</u>, or <u>I would become an English teacher</u>.

Compound-complex sentence, the not-so-basic variety (with main clauses underlined and the dependent clauses in italics), from Justin Kaplan's *Mrs. Clemens and Mark Twain*, first sentence of Chapter 7

"<u>Howells found it remarkable</u> *that none of the California writers who burst on the literary scene after the Civil War wanted to go back there*; <u>some of them even seemed to hate California</u>, *as if their frontier image of it was the only one they could accept.*"

The underlined parts are the two main clauses or sentences. The italicized parts need comment:

1. "that none of the California writers wanted to go back there" (an adverb clause modifying "remarkable") is interrupted with "who burst on the literary scene after the Civil War," an adjective clause modifying "writers."

2. "as if their frontier image of it was the only one" is an adverb clause modifying "seemed to hate."

3. "they could accept" is an adjective clause modifying "one." Notice the introductory "that" has been omitted.

Task 20

The following sentences are to be identified by type:

    A. Simple sentence
    B. Complex sentence
    C. Compound sentence
    D. Compound-complex sentence

(Answers are on page 176.)

1. After letting the grass grow for several weeks, Walter Petroskey called Chem-Lawn to help him out.

2. On Fifth Avenue, Rosalie Milano walked past the lions outside the New York Public Library; she was looking for her husband who had ducked into a bar.

3. Ecstatic, Tony Milano sat glowing on the bar stool because the Mets had just finished shutting out the Cubs.

4. The prom committee cancelled the dance because of the blizzard.

5. Michelle LeQuire and Marcy Milano work as trapeze artists: Michelle holds the record for the greatest number of flips, and Marcy is the only one ever with one hand to catch a hurling body.

6. Capital punishment many disagree with, but proponents say the *Bible* promotes "an eye for an eye," and "a tooth for a tooth."

7. Sandra Petroskey, who had never baked anything before, won first place in the Betty Crocker baking contest.

8. If Wanda Hughes married Henry Kissinger, she would be "Wanda Hughes Kissinger ⸱ now."

9. Matthew Mulvey came in first against twenty-five other contestants in a golf match for toddlers, and his brother Jonathan won the shot-put event on the same day.

10. In 1928 my father had a chance to buy the Dupont mansion at the end of Spring Rock Road in Branford, but because he was selfish, he spent the money on himself.

Task 20A

Practice writing the different types of sentences. Have your instructor check your work. (No answers are given.) Use the following sentences as guides:

1. Aimee Lynn Carroll earned the right to become a member of The National Honor Society. (Simple sentence with one verb, "earned" and one subject, "Aimee Carroll")

2. When some of the producers of *Dancing with the Stars* saw Eric Weiss dancing at his wedding, they asked him to appear on the show. (Complex sentence with an introductory adverb (subordinate) clause and a main clause following the comma)

3. Dan Carroll works in New York City, but he lives on Fence Creek Road near the osprey nest in the swamp. (Compound sentence separated with a comma and a conjunction)

4. Janis Carroll orchestrates magnificent galas, but Dan Carroll, who entertains his friends at these fetes with some rather tall stories, acts more like a guest than a host. (Compound/complex sentence with two main clauses and one subordinate clause)

Coordination and Subordination

To coordinate or to subordinate, that is the question. With apologies to Shakespeare aside, the writer faces a problem: What to emphasize, what not to emphasize so that the reader will know exactly what the writer intends.

These are the elements that may be coordinated (see Chapter 11)—words, phrases, clauses, and sentences (main clauses); these may be subordinated also, but this category needs some follow-up (see Chapter 13). For this chapter, concentration will focus on clauses.

The following coordinating conjunctions join main clauses: and, but, or, nor, for, and yet (with the comma after the conjunction).

Dan Robert Cole helps his father grow and sell vegetables and fruit, <u>and</u> they both enjoy reading grammar books.

Frank Anthony LaPila once owned Durham High School, <u>but</u> the teachers loved him anyhow.

The following correlative conjunctions join two main clauses only: both . . . and, not only . . . but also, whether . . . or, either . . . or, and neither . . . nor (usually with no comma).

Gee Collins <u>not only</u> reconditions houses <u>but also</u> reigns as Scrabble champion of East Guilford.

<u>Whether</u> Judi Hertz missed her bus <u>or</u> she deliberately slept in, no one is sure.

With semicolons but not with commas, the following connectives can be used to introduce the next clause: consequently, however, in fact, moreover, subsequently, in addition, also, indeed, then, nevertheless, therefore, and in contrast.

Ronald John Soja has little musical aptitude; <u>however</u>, his son does and teaches music at Daniel Hand High School.

Shannon Hornack flew to her new job in California; <u>consequently</u>, she had to sell her prized Jaguar.

Any one of the following subordinating conjunctions, placed at the beginning of a main clause, subordinates that clause and makes it now "less important," although still adding interesting facts to the sentence. Some of these subordinating conjunctions function as prepositions. "Before," for example, can be either a preposition or an introductory adverb, depending upon how "before" is used): after, although, as, as far as, as long as, as soon as, as if, because, before, even if, even though, if, inasmuch as, insofar as, provided that, since, so that, that, though, until, unless, when, whenever, where, wherever, whereas, while, and why.

Cindy Hornack misses her daughter <u>because</u> they were very close.
<u>Although</u> Bob Heifetz has lived in East Lyme for several years and now lives in Delaware, he still retains his New York accent.

Notice how "before," in the following examples, is used differently; the first use is as a subordinating conjunction, and the second is as a preposition.

<u>Before</u> Paula Chabot taught Latin for several years, she had played soccer for a professional team.
<u>Before</u> playing soccer, she had attended graduate school.

The problem: When is a main clause (see Chapter 4) appropriate and when is a subordinate clause (see also Chapter 4) appropriate? Obviously, the answer lies with the writer, who should know the differences between these handy elements.

Let's pose a problem and write a compound sentence and discuss whether or not to subordinate one (or more) of the clauses.

EXAMPLE

COMPOUND: St. Mark's Square in Venice floods during full and new moon tides, and tourists and locals use raised walkways to keep their feet dry.

Two **simple sentences** together, related, and meaningful, and grammatically equal, joined by a coordinating conjunction and a comma. But do I want to keep writing compound sentences all the time? Could these two related sentences be combined to make one complex sentence? The answer, of course, is yes.

COMPLEX: When St. Mark's Square in Venice floods during full and new moon tides, tourists and locals use raised walkways to keep their feet dry.

Of course, the choice of edition depends on the *context*, but certainly there is a choice here. With the compound sentence example, the author implies that both statements are of equal value, about the flooding and the raised walkways. However, in the complex sentence example, the author implies that the flooding becomes an interesting detail, subordinate to people using the raised walkways, stressed because of the main clause. "When," attached to the first clause, subordinates.

Or construct a simple sentence from the example.

SIMPLE: Tourists and locals use raised walkways to keep their feet dry in St. Mark's Square in Venice during full and new moon tides.

The complex sentence seems better in this case because emphasis may be given to the raised walkways and tourists or to the flooding in St. Mark's Square.

When writers coordinate or subordinate ideas, they must use the proper forms of coordination or subordination.

Relationships in Compound Sentences

"And" shows addition, something added, "but" indicates an opposite thought is about to happen, "or" signals an alternative to the first thought, "nor" indicates a negative alternative thought is about to follow, "for" shows a reason for the first thought or clause, and "yet" indicates another opposite thought about to follow.

EXAMPLES

- *and*—My father wrote for the *New Haven Register*, and my mother sometimes proofread some of his articles. (an addition)

- *but*—Newport authorities scheduled the fireworks for the night of the Fourth, but the rain forced the festivities to be cancelled. (negative following positive)

- *or*—The CEO of Philip Morris told his employees not to smoke in the building, or they would face disciplinary measures. (alternative)

- *nor*—Arthur Dimmesdale remained oblivious to Chillingworth's scrutiny, nor did he realize the physical change he himself was going through. (alternative negative)

- *for*—Gatsby threw lavish parties, for he desperately wanted to see Daisy Buchanan show up at one of them. (reason following)

- *yet*—Emily Dickinson knew much about worldly matters, yet she rarely left her home in Amherst, Massachusetts. (negative following positive)

Relationships in Complex Sentences

time

after, as long as, as soon as, before, since, until, when, whenever, while

<u>Until</u> the current problem is controlled, priests will suffer constant scrutiny for years to come.

condition

if, when, provided that, unless

The Mets need more pitching <u>if</u> they want to make a run for the pennant this year.

contrast

although, even though, though, while, whereas

<u>Even though</u> my class rank was low, I was accepted to four colleges.

degree

as far as, inasmuch as, insofar as

<u>Inasmuch as</u> Mike Piazza tried, he still had difficulty throwing out runners.

place

where, wherever

<u>Wherever</u> Billy Contois goes, he possesses an aura that is not easy to miss.

cause

because, since, as

Psychics on television have great success with their predictions <u>because</u> they ask the right questions.

Task 21

The following pairs of sentences after each number are closely related. You are to decide the best way to combine them and produce either a compound sentence or a complex sentence. There are no right or wrong answers, but make sure you clearly show the relationship between each pair. The order of the pairs may be reversed. (Suggested answers appear on pages 176–177.)

1. Reverend Arthur Dimmesdale tortured himself over his sins.
   Hester Prynne changed the significance of the scarlet "A" from "Adulteress" to "Angel."

2. Mike Piazza helped the Mets offensively but not defensively.
   Al Leiter added defensive power and clubhouse spirit to the pitching staff.

3. Choosing a computer ranks as a difficult task for the beginner.
   Adding needed programs boggles the minds of advanced users.

4. Educators every five years propose earthshaking plans.
   Taxpayers usually have no voice in the matter.

5. Harvesting swordfish demands a focused mentality.
   The Perfect Storm and *The Hungry Ocean* describe the techniques of swordfishing in detail.

6. A student can always find help with vocabulary.
   J. I. Rodale's *The Synonym Finder* or one of the thesauri is a necessary tool.

7. Being cool applies to most teenagers.
   Being studious does not apply to most teenagers.

8. The Irish economy of today no longer resembles that of the fifties.
   More computers and computer chips come from Ireland than from any other country.

9. Boat owners study weather reports more than do car owners.
   Cars are easier to take care of than boats are.

10. Babe Ruth at his best earned eighty thousand dollars a year.
    Players today set records with the amount of salary received.

Conclusion

When is a main clause appropriate and when is a subordinate clause appropriate? Obviously, the answer lies with the writer, who should know the differences between these handy elements.

Reference of Pronouns

Pronouns take the place of nouns (see Chapter 2), and for every noun, there exists a pronoun. Also, the word to which a pronoun refers is called an antecedent. All pronouns must refer precisely to another noun in the sentence or paragraph. Another way: Every pronoun one uses in a text must stand for or rename a noun. Otherwise a *reference of pronoun* error occurs. Most of the time, the reader can guess the reference even though it (the reference) might be unclear; sometimes, however, the reader has no clue. There are four types of reference of pronoun error: ambiguous reference, general reference, weak reference, and indefinite reference.

Ambiguous Reference

Ambiguous reference occurs when a pronoun refers to more than one antecedent. The reader has no clue what the pronoun means.

Mary told her mother she was crazy.

Your mind can rationalize who is "crazy" in this sentence. At one time the crazy one is the mother; at another time the crazy one is Mary. Therefore, one pronoun in this sentence (in this case "she"; there is nothing unclear about "her," referring to Mary) is ambiguous or unclear, because "she" is referring to or renaming two nouns ("Mary" and "mother") in the same sentence. To correct this example:

Mary thought her mother was crazy.

OR

Mary said, "Mother, I'm crazy."

OR

Mary said, "Mother, you're crazy."

General Reference

General reference occurs when a pronoun (which, that, this, and it) refers to the general idea preceding it, but not to any specific word.

After volunteers counted and recounted the ballots in key Florida counties, still no President was elected, which caused both Bush and Gore to file lawsuits claiming victory.

At first glance, one might say there is no mistake here. However, "which" is a relative pronoun but does not relate to or rename a word in this sentence. "Which" does refer, in general, to the "counting of ballots," but it is not specific and is therefore termed a general reference error. This error usually occurs with "which," "this," or "that," and sometimes "it"; also, general references of pronouns abound in all sorts of writing, but these errors should be avoided.

CORRECTION: After volunteers counted and recounted the ballots in key Florida counties, still no President was elected; therefore, both Bush and Gore filed lawsuits claiming victory.

Another example,

Billy Contois sometimes works out at the gym twice a day, which makes a healthy specimen, unlike the "terminator."

First of all, "which" is next to day and should modify it. But "which" refers, in general, to Billy's working out at the gym, sometimes twice a day. "Which" must refer to a single word rather than to a general idea. Correcting this sentence is easy:

Because Billy Contois sometimes works out twice a day at the gym, he is a healthy specimen. (Notice: "which" has been removed from the sentence.)

Weak Reference

Weak reference of pronouns, the lack of an antecedent, although not very common, does happen.

Our fishing vacation took us to Lake Ontario, but we had a difficult time finding them.

This sentence might or might not make sense, but the pronoun "them" has no word to hold on to. "Them" obviously refers to fish, but the word "fish" is not there. "Fishing" is, but "fishing" is a participle, an adjective, modifying "vacation." Therefore, a pronoun that has no word to relate to falls under the category of weak reference of pronoun. Another example,

I searched the creeks of the golf course but did not find any.

Of course (no pun intended), "any" refers to "golf balls."

Indefinite Reference

The final category is *indefinite reference*. Look at the following example:

They say smoking is injurious to one's health. Who says? This example, therefore, is an example of indefinite reference of pronouns. "They" could stand for "doctors," "parents," or even "teachers." Certainly "they" demands a plural noun.

Does this rule eliminate such favorites as "Is it supposed to snow on Thursday," or the beginning of a good story, "It all began on the night of . . ."? Most likely not, because these expressions belong to our *informal language*; they should not, however, be used in formal essays, tests, or any place else that calls for formal language.

Task 22

Try your hand at recognizing the reference of pronoun in the following examples. Then rewrite the sentences (the best way is to try writing the sentences without the pronouns, but if you do use a pronoun, make sure the reference is correct. Keep in mind, some of the sentences will be correct.

Place a "C" next to the correct ones.
Use "A" for ambiguous.
Use "B" for general.
Use "D" for weak.
Use "E" for indefinite.
(Answers are on pages 177–178.)

1. My cousin brought his glove to the Mets–Yankee game because he anticipated catching a few in the left field bleachers.

2. Our tour guide in Italy said a few things negative about Americans which made some tourists on the trip angry.

3. Phil introduced me to his cousin who pitched for the New Britain Roc-Cats.

4. Unless recreational anglers stand up for their rights, they may lose their impact on politicians.

5. In the paper the other day, it said that the annual Shellfish Festival was canceled because the clams and oysters rotted.

6. The local building committee proposed a new high school that would accommodate 1,200 students, that would house an Olympic-size pool, and that would cost 48 million dollars. That made me vote against the proposal.

7. When the teacher asked her prize pupil an easy question, he amazed the class with his insensitivity.

8. When the rain continued for several days, it made me find indoor activities.

9. School busses hold up traffic unnecessarily, but the students don't care because they usually arrive late anyway.

10. As the pitcher rubbed the baseball with resin, it caused the next pitch to drop sharply into the strike zone.

REVIEWING CHAPTERS 8 AND 9

Task 23

The following sentences are either correct, or have a reference of pronoun error or are coordinated or subordinated incorrectly. Identify the error; if the sentence is correct, place a "C" next to the number; use "A" for reference of pronouns and "B" for incorrect subordination or coordination. (Answers are on pages 178–179.)

1. Although you use the thesaurus regularly, your vocabulary will increase.

2. Transparencies help the presenter clarify some technical points, and they are difficult to use.

3. Fred Lynn and Lynn Swann roomed together at USC, and both later played in professional all-star games in baseball and football respectively.

4. After the *Titanic* had rammed an iceberg, the captain said that it was in the wrong place at the wrong time.

5. Officials at Madison Square Garden announced that ticket prices for the following year would be reduced by fifteen percent, which pleased the season ticket holders.

6. Captain Ahab mesmerized his crew into thinking that their main objective was to capture Moby Dick, and Starbuck, the first mate, strongly objected.

7. When Bret Harte visited Mark Twain in Hartford, he would get roaring drunk and smoke all the cigars in the house.

8. Male ospreys guard their nests from afar while the female osprey sits on the nest to hatch the eggs.

9. Hermit crabs last only hours in brackish water, and green crabs last much longer.

10. It will be a cold day in July when my uncle lets me use his boat.

Agreement: Subject-Verb, Pronoun-Antecedent

If anything needs emphasis, agreement does. The rules are simple: Every *verb* (in number—that is, singular or plural) must agree with its *subject* (see Chapter 5); every *pronoun* must agree with its *antecedent*. The simplicity overwhelms. Let's start with subject-verb.

Subject-Verb Agreement

Agreement between subject and verb poses a problem in two tenses only: the present and the present perfect. Look at the following conjugation of the verb "promise."

Person	Singular	Plural
	Present	
First person	I promise	we promise
Second person	you promise	you promise
Third person	he, she, it promises	they promise
	Present Perfect	
First person	I have promised	we have promised
Second person	you have promised	you have promised
Third person	he, she, it has promised	they have promised

In both these tenses, the third person singular has a changed form with an "-s" ending, but the plural does not change its form; also, the second and third persons remain constant with no change. In other words, there is agreement between subject and verb.

With "ordinary" singular and plural nouns, there rarely exists a problem of agreement:

When Johan Santana <u>pitches</u>, the Mets usually <u>win</u>. (The subordinate verb "pitches" is singular because the subject (Johan Santana) is singular; the main verb "win" is plural because the subject, "Mets" is plural.)

Sparks <u>fly</u> when Peter Weiss <u>uses</u> a knife and fork. (The main verb "fly" is plural because "sparks" is plural; the subordinate verb "uses" is singular because "Peter Weiss" is singular.)

Problems arise, however, because there are some words that almost defy logic and cause students and teachers headaches. These pose the "special problems" of subject-verb agreement.

SPECIAL PROBLEMS OF SUBJECT-VERB AGREEMENT

1. Using "either . . . or" and "neither . . . nor."

    a. If these correlatives join singular subjects, the verb must be singular: Either my **sister** or my **brother** <u>visits</u> China every year.
    b. If these correlatives join plural subjects, the verb must be plural: In the Olympics, neither the **Chinese** nor the **Americans** <u>compete</u> well against the Russians.
    c. If these correlatives join a singular noun with a plural noun, the verb agrees with the noun closest to it.

Neither **Jake** nor his **brothers** <u>play</u> the violin.
Either the 60,000 **fans** or the public address **announcer** <u>misunderstands</u> the official score's ruling.

2. Nouns joined by "and" govern a plural verb.

Respectability and contentment <u>accompany</u> old age.
Blocking for the quarterback **and carrying** the ball <u>are</u> two requirements of fullbacks.

3. The verb should not be affected by a phrase between the subject and verb.

The **faculty**, as well as many of the students, <u>does</u> not <u>understand</u> the new attendance policy. (Subject and verb are both singular.)
The **space** between the two cars <u>allows</u> no room for opening doors. (Both subject and verb are singular.)

4. Using "a number of" or "the number of"

   a. As a subject, "a number" followed by "of" takes a plural verb: **A number of** travelers in the Southwest <u>have</u> witnessed UFOs.
   b. As a subject, "the number" followed by "of" takes a singular verb: **The number of** different ideas admen can generate <u>astounds</u> me.

5. The following pronouns are singular: another, anybody, anyone, anything, each, either, everybody, everyone, everything, much, neither, nobody, no one, nothing, one, other, someone, something, somebody. Therefore they take a singular verb.

Each of the books <u>is</u> over a thousand pages long.
Anything my brother accomplishes <u>astonishes</u> me.
Nobody <u>has</u> the right to take another's life.

6. The following pronouns are plural: several, few, many, others, both.

Several of the contestants <u>know</u> most of the answers.
A **few** in the audience <u>were</u> enthusiastic.
Many of the pages <u>were</u> torn.
Both of the twins <u>attend</u> Providence College.

7. The following pronouns are singular or plural, depending on what follows them: some, none, most, all.

Some of the movies on Channel 8 <u>were</u> funny. (plural because of "movies")
Some of the cake <u>was</u> left over. (singular because of "cake")
None of my professors <u>like</u> me. (plural because of "professors")
None of the field <u>was</u> plowed. (singular because of "field")
Most of my friends <u>are</u> loyal. (plural because of "friends")
Most of the food <u>was</u> gone. (singular because of "food")
All of books in the library <u>were</u> damaged. (plural because of "books")
All of the time <u>was</u> spent in mourning. (singular because of "time")

The word "none" conjures up Miss Thistlebottom, Theodore M. Bernstein's fictitious epitome of strictness, who told her students, " 'None' is always singular." Bernstein's explanation is paraphrased here: "None" is singular when followed by a singular noun. "None," therefore, is plural when followed by a plural. However, if the writer (the careful one) considers singularity, as in "not one," then "none" is singular. There should be no question about "some," "most," or "all." The number of these words is determined by the noun that follows them.

8. Collective nouns are singular in form and usually take a singular verb.

The **pod** (of whales) <u>clusters</u> around the biggest male for protection.
The **wedge** (of geese flying) <u>moves</u> precisely south.
That **choir** <u>sings</u> beautifully.

Exceptions to this rule occur when the writer thinks of the elements of the collective noun as individuals rather than as a group:

The **Board of Education** <u>flounder</u> during budget considerations.
As the **gaggle** (of geese on the ground) <u>waddle</u> here and there, <u>they</u> make a mess. (The pronoun must agree, also.)

Pronoun-Antecedent Agreement

Pronouns must agree with their antecedents in both number and gender. Also, pronouns should be placed as closely as possible to the antecedent.

After **Erin Mulvey** had bought <u>her</u> new **Mercedes**, <u>she</u> drove <u>it</u> to California and back.
Although **Kevin Walsh** acquired a huge **amount of cash** in a short time, <u>he</u> never told where he procured <u>it</u>.

SPECIAL PROBLEMS OF PRONOUN-ANTECEDENT AGREEMENT

1. The indefinite pronouns listed under Number 5 in "Special Problems of Subject-Verb Agreement" need a singular pronoun.

Anyone can succeed if <u>she</u> tries.
Everyone brought a gift for <u>his</u> contribution to the poor.
Someone should admit <u>his</u> guilt.

2. Plural indefinite pronouns require plural pronouns.

Several of the participants quit because <u>they</u> were tired.
A few in the front row had <u>their</u> tickets checked.
I kept my seat on the bus, but **others** had to change <u>theirs</u>.

3. Those indefinite pronouns that are either singular or plural take singular or plural pronouns accordingly.

Some of the line twisted <u>itself</u> around the prop. (Both pronoun and antecedent are singular because of "line.")

None of the students had <u>their</u> pencils with <u>them</u>. (Both pronoun and antecedent are plural because of "students.")

Task 24

Try correcting some of the following agreement problems. There are a few correct ones to keep you guessing. (Answers are on page 179.)

1. The psychology of athletics demand physical as well as mental endurance for each athlete.

2. Neither Josey nor the rest of the class was responsible for the substitute teacher's breakdown.

3. There was placed in our midst replicas of two ancient cities, and we were to compare and contrast two civilizations based on our findings.

4. The only refuge we had were the two cabins not far from Mt. Washington.

5. The United States Supreme Court are agreed that the Florida State Legislature should demand a recount of ballots from several counties.

6. Every Senator promised to accomplish great feats for their individual state.

7. Winning the lottery and then basking in the sun on Aruba dominates my every thought.

8. Heard on Monday Night Football: "These kind of backs are a dime a dozen."

9. None of the leaves in my yard ever blows onto my neighbor's yard, as he constantly implies.

10. Captain Ahab, as well as Starbuck, Stubb, Flask, and the rest of the crew, attack whales as if the leviathans had personally insulted the *Pequod*.

11. Some of my favorite passages from *Moby Dick*: the rescue of Tashtego by Queequeg, Fleece's sermon to the sharks, Ahab's first speech to his crew, and the third day chase of the white whale provides me with enough to think about during slow times.

Task 25

Some of the following sentences contain errors in coordination or subordination, reference of pronouns, or agreement between subject-verb or pronoun-antecedent. Identify the error by placing "B," "C," or "D" next to the number, and rewrite the sentence. If the sentence is correct, place an "A" next to the number. (Answers are on pages 179–180.)

A—Sentence is correct.
B—Sentence is incorrectly coordinated or subordinated.
C—Sentence contains a reference of pronoun mistake.
D—Sentence has an agreement problem.

1. The moratoria imposed by the DEP on blackfish and striped bass has increased the numbers of both species.

2. To be considered a "keeper" in Connecticut, fluke must measure seventeen inches or more, which most anglers agree with.

3. They say that Newport is a drinking town with a sailing problem.

4. Roger Angell, E. B. White's stepson, writes about baseball better than any other writer.

5. Physics baffle me because of the intricacies one must study.

6. The boss said the other day that if everyone were to do their jobs, this place would be a better working environment.

7. John Irving's new book, *The Fourth Hand*, promises to enthrall readers; moreover, this work will never sell as many copies as *The World According to Garp*.

8. When Mickey Mantle and Roger Maris battled for the home run crown in 1961, the media told the public that the two sluggers were feuding daily.

9. During his Introduction to Literature 101 course, Gerry Degenhardt told one of the students that he was about to leave for the office.

10. Florindo Frank "Porky" Vieira, the former baseball coach at the University of New Haven, put on clinics that helped youngsters become excellent players.

11

Parallel Structure

One of the ways students can improve their writing is to use **parallel structure*** when the text demands the use of a **coordinating conjunction** (and, but, or, nor, for, yet) to join **words**, **phrases**, or **clauses**; also, when the text demands items in a series (three or more); and finally when the text demands the use of **correlative conjunctions** (either . . . or, neither . . . nor, not only . . . but also, whether . . . or, both . . . and). In each of these three cases, the writer is obligated to "express himself in the same ("parallel" does mean similar) grammatical form," pairing or serializing **participles** with participles, **infinitive phrases** with infinitive phrases, and so on. Parallel structure is also effective with comparisons.

Using *parallel structure* consists of expressing oneself using like grammatical terms. Definitions like this always baffle students until they understand "like grammatical terms." Here is an easy example: Prevent dust buildup <u>by cleaning your tape deck monthly</u> and <u>dust your house weekly</u>. We see that something is wrong here, besides the awkward construction, because "by cleaning your tape deck monthly" and "dust your house weekly" are unlike grammatical terms. The first, technically, is a gerund phrase used as an object of the preposition "by"; the second is a verb and its direct object (and modifier). Untechnically, the two grammatical terms do not match. Further untechnically, "cleaning" and "dust" do not look alike because one is missing the "-ing."

CORRECTIONS: Prevent dust buildup by <u>cleaning your tape deck monthly</u> and by <u>dusting your house weekly</u>. (two matching gerund phrases)

OR

Prevent dust buildup: <u>Clean your tape deck monthly</u>, and <u>dust your house weekly</u>. (two imperative sentences)

Let's look at an even easier example:

I love <u>to read</u> and <u>writing.</u> (The **infinitive,** "to read" is paired with a **gerund,** "writing.")

*Words in boldface have been defined and explored in previous chapters.

THE OBVIOUS CORRECTION: I love <u>to read</u> and <u>(to) write</u>.

Note: Usage tells us that it is permissible to leave the "to" of the infinitive off.

OR

I love <u>reading</u> and <u>writing</u>.

Let's try a more complicated sentence: Robert Brock Harris has participated in not only <u>the Big Brother Program</u> but also <u>in the Rathskellers</u>. On first glimpse, this sentence seems OK, but there is a minor flaw. The correlatives "not only" and "but also" have two different sentence elements following them. First, "the Big Brother Program" is a proper noun with "the"; however, "in the Rathskellers" is a prepositional phrase.

There are two ways to correct this sentence:

Robert Brock Harris has participated in not only <u>the Big Brother Program</u> but also <u>the Rathskellers</u>.

Robert Brock Harris has participated not only <u>in the Big Brother Program</u> but also <u>in the Rathskellers</u>.

The differences between the wrong version and the two corrected versions at first does not seem apparent unless we underline the correct parts and contrast them with the original poor sentence. The change is subtle.

Using Coordinating Conjunctions in Parallel Structure

The following are the only *coordinating conjunctions* you will ever need: and, but, or, nor, for, yet. "Coordinating" means equivalent, or synonymous. When a coordinating conjunction is used, whatever structures the conjunction joins, those elements must be the same grammatical form. These coordinating conjunctions join words with words, phrases with phrases, clauses with clauses, and sentences with sentences.

WORDS: <u>morosely</u> and <u>glumly</u> (two adverbs); <u>clawing</u> and <u>ripping</u> (two participles or gerunds depending on their use); <u>miserable</u> but <u>content</u> (two adjectives); <u>feast</u> or <u>famine</u> (two nouns), <u>firm</u> yet <u>fair</u> (two adjectives).

PHRASES: <u>dishing up fantastic recipes</u> but <u>leaving a mess</u> (two participial or gerund phrases, depending on their use); <u>to crash the party</u> or <u>to stay at home</u> (two infinitive phrases); <u>down in the river</u> or <u>up in the sky</u> (two adverbs with prepositional phrases modifying them)

CLAUSES: <u>That the pitcher fooled Casey by the pitch</u> or <u>that the umpire miscalculated the strike zone</u> caused the fans in Mudville to scream (two noun clauses);

The lawyer, who had impressed the jury and who later won the case was later arrested for fraud (two adjective clauses); Because Ichabod Crane suspected everyone or because he was superstitious, his entire existence in Sleepy Hollow became paranoia (two adverb clauses).

SENTENCES: *Moby Dick* ranks as one of America's greatest novels, but Melville suffered from anonymity when it was first published. Monument Mountain in Manchester, Vermont, serves as a testimony to the greatness of early American writers, yet few Vermonters know who those writers are.

Note: Coordinating conjunctions connecting sentences usually demand a comma before the conjunction. Short sentences connected with conjunctions may or may not need a comma, depending upon whether the relationship is obvious. Zee Leach loves to walk to the store but Martin Leach likes to drive. (No comma is needed because the two sentences are obviously connected.)

Items (words, phrases, clauses, and sentences) in a series (three or more) demand the use of parallel structure.

WORDS IN A SERIES

Most sophomores consider standardized tests impossible, useless, and a waste of time. This sentence, although a sweeping generalization, still carries meaning, but there is something radically wrong because "waste of time" is a noun with a prepositional phrase while "impossible" and "useless" are adjectives. The sentence is easily corrected: Most sophomores consider standardized tests impossible, useless, and wasteful. (Now, there are three adjectives.)

Tony Jenkins considers himself the perfect father, the ideal husband, and the world's most enthusiastic Baltimore Oriole fan. (Notice how these noun phrases fit nicely into the sentence, even the last one, which has several modifiers but matches the other two phrases.)

CONCLUSION: When words are in a series and usually separated by commas, those words must have the same grammatical form.

PHRASES IN A SERIES

Prepositional, gerund, participial, and infinitive phrases by simple definition are groups of words that do not contain a verb, although the last three will have words resembling verbs (the reason for the designation of **verbal**). When verbals are used in a series, each item must be the same, grammatically, as the others.

PREPOSITIONAL PHRASE

Over the river, through the woods, and climbing the steep mountain, we trekked to grandmother's house.

What's wrong here? "Over the river" and "through the woods" are prepositional phrases, but "climbing the steep mountain" is a participial phrase. An argument might arise: But they are all adjectives! True, but they are not the right kind. Since the writer began his series with two prepositional phrases, he is obligated to add a third prepositional phrase (or fourth, or fifth, etc.) The sentence should look like this:

Over the river, through the woods, and up the mountain we trekked to grandmother's house.

GERUND (NOUN) PHRASES

Rushing the quarterback, protecting their own quarterback, and when they recovered a fourth quarter fumble won the game for the Colts. (Here are two **gerund** phrases paired with an **adverb clause**.)
Rushing the quarterback, protecting their own quarterback, and recovering a fourth quarter fumble won the game for the Colts. (now, three gerunds as the subjects)

PARTICIPIAL PHRASES

Captain Ahab, pacing the deck, while he was exhorting his crew, and seeking only one thing, turned the *Pequod* into a nightmare for the mates and the crew. (Here is an adverb clause sandwiched between two participial phrases)
Captain Ahab, pacing the deck, exhorting his crew, and seeking only one thing, turned the *Pequod* into a nightmare for the mates and the crew. (Now, three participial phrases modifying "Captain Ahab.")

Notice the difference in the two previous sentences. In the gerund sentence, the "-ing" phrases are **subjects—nouns**. In the second, the "-ing" phrases modify "Captain Ahab" and are therefore **participial phrases, adjectives**. Notice that participles end in "-ing," "-d," "-ed," "-n," "-en," and "-t." There is even one that ends in "-m" (swum) and another in "-g" (hung).

INFINITIVE PHRASES

Infinitive phrases are the most complicated only because they can be used as nouns, adjectives, or adverbs.

NOUNS: <u>To sit through a boring lecture</u>, to <u>experience a teacher with a monotone</u>, or <u>to watch the grass grow</u> makes one itchy. (These infinitive phrases are subjects of the verb "makes.")

ADJECTIVES: Mary Ann Coe Trinker developed a plan <u>to use the family car more conservatively</u>, to open a bank account, and <u>to budget better for vacations</u>. (The infinitive phrase modifies "Kathy Bruyette.")

ADVERBS: For punishment, I was made <u>to sit in the corner</u>, <u>to read a grammar book</u>, and <u>to write volumes</u>. (These infinitive phrases modify the verb "was made.")

CLAUSES IN A SERIES

Three authors who used clauses strung together in series—Victor Hugo (who supposedly wrote the longest sentence ever—50,000 words), Herman Melville, and Ralph Waldo Emerson—were masters of their craft and educated in the Classic tradition, which demanded the knowledge of grammar in many languages. They seemed to know that a part of speech was not just a word, but could be a large group of words that contained a verb and for the most part even looked like a sentence. Average writers should also use clauses to give variety to their writing.

ADJECTIVE CLAUSES: The crew of the *Andrea Gail* was composed of men <u>who drank great quantities of beer on land</u>, <u>who lived wildly while not at sea</u>, but <u>who knew their business and toiled bravely in the terrible conditions of the Bering Sea.</u>

NOUN CLAUSES: <u>That Joe Dimaggio connected himself to the Mafia</u>, <u>that he carried the Yankees to a record number of World Series wins</u>, and <u>that he attracted the most beautiful women in the world</u> define him as a complicated character.

ADVERB CLAUSES: Ethan Frome reigns as an unforgettable literary figure <u>because he married for the wrong reason</u>, <u>because he "unsecretly" fell in love with his wife's live-in cousin</u>, and <u>because he failed in a double-suicide attempt</u>.

SENTENCES IN A SERIES

Sentences in a series comprise compound sentences. How many sentences can be strung together? The answer is simply as many as the writer wants, as many as he needs to convey ideas. "Series" implies three or more: Playing baseball requires superhuman dexterity, playing basketball requires superhuman endurance, and playing golf requires superhuman concentration. (This sentence has the possibility of adding several more sentences, independent clauses, to it.) Notice that after the first two sentences about baseball and then basketball, the writer is obligated to continue with a sentence (or two) so that this entire unit is parallel.

Using Correlative Conjunctions in Parallel Structure

The correlative conjunctions include either . . . or, neither . . . nor, not only . . . but also, both . . . and, whether . . . or. "Correlative" means that these pairs of words always go together and that they join two items only. To use these **correlative conjunctions** correctly, the writer must place the same grammatical forms after each word in the pair. For example,

Since the field trip has been postponed, the seniors will <u>either</u> *go to the auditorium* <u>or</u> *go to their homeroom.* (This sentence then contains parallel structure because the verb "go" follows both "either" and "or.") Another way of writing the same sentence:

Since the field trip has been postponed, the seniors will go <u>either</u> *to the auditorium* <u>or</u> *to their homeroom.* (This sentence, without repeating the word "go," is parallel because what follows "either" and "or" are prepositional phrases, "to the auditorium" and "to their homeroom.")

WORDS WITH CORRELATIVE CONJUNCTIONS

The beggar remained <u>not only</u> *calm* <u>but also</u> *cool* when the pedestrian made a disparaging comment. (two adjectives)

<u>Neither</u> *snow* <u>nor</u> *sleet* can keep the postman from his appointed rounds. (two nouns)

The next-door millionaire decided he would leave his fortune to <u>either</u> *him* <u>or</u> *me.* (two pronouns)

PHRASES WITH CORRELATIVE CONJUNCTIONS

Instant replay in the National Football League is popular <u>not only</u> *with the fans* <u>but also</u> *with the coaches.* (two prepositional phrases)

We prevented erosion in our backyard by <u>both</u> *digging a trench* <u>and</u> *rerouting the water.* (two gerund phrases)

<u>Whether</u> *sailing along the Thimble Islands* <u>or</u> *skiing down the slopes at Bromley,* my family always enjoys themselves. (two **participial phrases**)

Because the plane was low on fuel, the pilot did not know <u>whether</u> *to land on the highway beneath him* <u>or</u> *to try making the airport.* (two **infinitive phrases**)

CLAUSES WITH CORRELATIVE CONJUNCTIONS

Newport, Rhode Island, shines in the summer <u>not only</u> *because yachtsmen from all over the world bring their vessels to the harbor* <u>but also</u> *because the tourist trade is in full swing.* (two **adverb clauses**)

Because there was no clear distinction between the top ten scholars of the school, the academic prize went to <u>either</u> *whoever had the highest English score* <u>or</u> *whoever scored the best in math.* (two **noun clauses**)

Can **adjective clauses** be used with correlative conjunctions? There's no way; it's not possible.

Using **words**, **phrases**, **clauses**, and **sentences** in **parallel structure** shows maturity in writing and a definite grasp of grammar. A review of the terms shows just how much one needs to know to use parallel structure competently: **Noun (noun phrase, noun clause), adjective (adjective phrase, adjective clause), adverb (adverb phrase, adverb clause), coordinating conjunctions**, and **correlative conjunctions.**

Note: Using parallel structures clears up incorrect or silly comparisons.

One example that always comes to mind is a person writing about the high school football team: The Daniel Hand football tigers are better than Guilford. Simply put, the author here is comparing a high school team to the town of Guilford. "Guilford's team" would clear this sentence nicely.

Task 26

Try your hand at correcting some of the following sentences. Some are correct. Just rewrite the sentences that lack parallel structure. (Answers are on page 180.)

1. Emily Dickinson not only wrote beautiful poetry about nature but also about love, even though she was not attached to anyone.

2. The Reverend Dimmesdale in *The Scarlet Letter* ruined his chances of the great reward when he fell in love with Hester Prynne and when he denied involvement with her in front of a crowd.

3. *The Marble Faun* by Hawthorne is both a riveting murder mystery and holds the reader with a travelogue of many parts of Italy.

4. Fishing on the bottom for tautog is more exciting than bluefish.

5. E. L. Doctorow disappointed his readers with *Loon Lake* because no one really understood the premise and his agents did not efficiently promote the book.

6. Casting for striped bass requires a knowledge of the local waters, demands certain equipment, and getting up early when the bass are feeding.

7. Babe Ruth's granddaughter Linda lives in Durham, Connecticut, constantly promotes the Babe's positive image, but unfortunately never met her famous grandfather.

8. In the bartending world, mixologists reign as amateur psychologists, masters of recipes, and in general pretend to know everything.

9. When Mark Twain wrote *Huckleberry Finn*, he attempted three new ideas: sell the book in serial form, exploring dialects along the Mississippi River, and telling the story of a youngster coming of age.

10. Lenny Wilkens promised me that I could go to the shoot-around before the game, that he would buy lunch, and getting two free tickets to the Knicks and Raptors.

Task 27

Now that you have mastered parallel structure, correct the following sentences where parallel structure is mixed in with other errors. Place the correct letter next to the number on your paper and then rewrite the sentence if there is an error. (Answers are on pages 180–181).

A—Correct sentence
B—Lacking coordination or subordination
C—Reference of pronoun error
D—Agreement problem
E—Parallel structure error

1. I took a day off and searched the golf course, but I could not find any.

2. A bartender represents not only the management of the bar but also has a responsibility to the patrons.

3. In Norse Mythology, Aegir is the god of the sea, but in Roman mythology, Neptune is the god of the sea.

4. Although Robert Frost was born in San Francisco, he is known as the "New England Poet."

5. The President chastised the Secretary of State when he was reading the paper about taxes.

6. An accessory after the fact is a person who helps another avoid arrest after they have committed a crime.

7. When Macbeth was told that his wife had died, he thought that she should have waited for a more opportune time.

8. William Blake, who lived between the years of 1757 and 1827, won fame both as a mystic and illustrating some of his own works and those of others.

9. In 1945, Ray Milland won an Oscar for his performance in *The Lost Weekend*, but Joan Crawford won one too for her brilliant performance in *Mildred Pierce*.

10. Anyone who writes a resume must remember that they are presenting themselves on paper to their future employers.

11. The Financial News Network, as well as the Madison Square Garden Network and Cinemax, have their offices in New York.

12. For the best results, black sea bass, a delicacy in many Chinese restaurants, should be cooked whole.

13. Coyotes wreak havoc, especially with small house pets in wooded areas where animals are allowed to roam, which makes me fearful for my kitty.

14. On our annual trek to Newport, Rhode Island, one of the first stops is the Aquidnic Lobster Company to purchase the biggest lobsters available.

15. Success is counted sweetest by those who never succeed, by those who disregard the rules of etiquette, and anyone not listening.

Misplaced and Dangling Modifiers

Not only do *misplaced modifiers* lead the reader the wrong way, but they also sometimes cause humor where humor is far from intended. These modifiers usually sensibly modify something in the sentence but are too far away from that something, or they are next to a word they seem to modify but really do not. Look at the following examples.

Dennis Randall wandered through the streets of Rome out of sorts.

"Out of sorts" is misplaced because obviously "Rome" is the word modified or described. But the intent here was to describe Dennis as he wandered. Therefore the modifier is misplaced. Look at the correction:

Out of sorts, Dennis Randall wandered through the streets of Rome.

Now, "out of sorts" is next to the proper word; we have even changed "out of sorts" from an adjective (incorrectly modifying "Rome," a noun) to an adverb, modifying "wandered," showing "how he wandered."
Another example,

I met my future bride while temping for a vacationer from the French Embassy.

The problem here is that "temping for a vacationer from the French Embassy" could modify or describe "I" or "bride," because of its position. We rewrite the sentence:

While temping for a vacationer from the French Embassy, I met my future bride.

OR

I met my future bride while she was temping for a vacationer from the French Embassy.

One of the words that is constantly misplaced is "only." In the following sentence, notice how the meaning changes when "only" is moved around:

Only I have three days left before I go back to work. ("I" am the only one to have some vacation left.)

I *only* have three days left before I go back to work. (Placing "only" before "have" is meaningless. Better to leave "only" out in this case.)

I have *only* three days left before I go back to work. (The speaker bemoans the fact that in a mere three days the vacation is over.)

I have three days *only* left before I go back to work. ("Only," here, seems to conflict with "left." "Only" after "left" is out of the question.)

"Dangling" conjures up all sorts of snickers from some classes just as Emily Dickinson's "There is no frigate like a book" does. If grammarians had somehow thought about "dangling," they might have reconsidered and called this gaffe "the nowhere modifier" or "the useless modifier" or "the modifier that does not sensibly modify any other word in the sentence." Unlike the misplaced modifier, which can simply be moved into another position and be correct, the dangling modifier, which does not modify any word sensibly (and thus "dangles"), must be recast as a clause or the entire sentence must be revised.

EXAMPLES

Wanting to move closer to family and friends, the Yankees allowed Bobo Newsome to break his contract.

"Wanting to move closer to family and friends" in this sentence modifies (or describes) "the Yankees." This participial phrase really doesn't sensibly modify "Bobo Newsome" either because simply moving the phrase around causes awkwardness at best. Therefore the phrase dangles. Notice how clearly the example reads corrected:

The Yankees allowed Bobo Newsome to break his contract because he wanted to move closer to family and friends.

Another example:

Trying to get away from the extreme horror of the situation, the Great White Shark continued to tear his way up my right leg.

"Trying to get away . . . ," does not modify "the great white shark." There is no word that this participial phrase can hang onto. The phrase dangles.

CORRECTION: While I was trying to get away from the extreme horror of the situation, the great white shark continued to tear his way up my right leg.

Task 28

In the following sentences, first identify the error (misplaced or dangling modifier); then rewrite the sentence. If the sentence is correct, mark it with "C." (Answers are on pages 181–182.)

1. Based on the circumstantial evidence favoring his client, the lawyer assumed that the other party was guilty.

2. Rehearsing his difficult role, the actor practiced in front of a mirror for facial takes.

3. Al Gore, promising to work hard in office, never had a chance after he lost the electoral votes from Tennessee, his home state.

4. The professional photographer took pictures of everyone who walked by in an hour.

5. Approaching the runway on the outer portion eastward, the control tower ordered the SST to abandon the landing and try again.

6. Most anglers have at least one broken fishing rod around the house that could be converted into an ice fishing jigging rod.

7. When responding to Nick after Nick had said, "You can't repeat the past," Gatsby said, "Of course you can."

8. Emptying the garbage or washing the kitchen floor, these chores bother me the most.

9. Scientists at the University of Georgia have isolated a way to identify members of fish families by analyzing their ear bones.

10. Tagging striped bass for conservation purposes, The Littoral Society of New Jersey has done an excellent job reviving the bass population.

Task 29

In the following sentences, misplaced and dangling modifiers have been added to the scheme of things. You know the routine by now:

A—Correct sentence
B—Lacking coordination or subordination
C—Reference of pronoun error
D—Agreement problem
E—Parallel structure error
F—Misplaced or dangling modifer

(Answers are on page 182.)

1. However, Harvard couldn't bust up what was called for—a drop kick—and (Albie) Booth, with the coolness that has characterized his play on all occasions, stepped back to the 16 yard-line, took the snap from center, and kicked.

2. In 1939, at Jack Schneider's Pants Shop on Chapel Street in New Haven, one could buy a pair of woolen slacks for $2.95 and they could get a second pair for $1.00.

3. In 1939 at Kaysey's Restaurant, a lobster luncheon including fries, rolls, and drawn butter cost only fifty cents, which one could not come close to today.

4. While frolicking on the playground, the teacher on duty reprimanded the youth for being reckless.

5. Some of the movie were funny, but the directors miscast several of the stars.

6. The gam in the middle of the ocean between two whaling ships were common in the nineteenth century.

7. Jack Davis, who is not only a world-recognized psychiatrist but he is also an accomplished artist, ran the Grove School in Madison, Connecticut.

8. As he ran along the last mile in the town of Biloxi near the supermarket of the six-mile race, Larry O'Shea Jr. felt a pang in his side.

9. Kevin and Brenda Walsh love to socialize with their friends, adore going to the movies, and look forward to camping out with their children.

10. Richard Wright, who wrote *Native Son* and *Black Boy*, is one of my favorite authors.

11. Diane Wiknik Andrews, along with several of her classmates, plan the best reunions.

12. Archie and Faye Erskine travel to Florida every year to visit their friends and play golf with them.

13. Tim Malone thinks of himself as a great fisherman, and the only things he catches regularly is old boots.

14. Horoscopes are written in such sweeping generalities that they are bound to get something right.

15. Mystery novels keep me in suspense, but I am bored by historical novels.

Sentence Variety

A good writer varies his sentences just as a good dresser varies his attire. True, in school many of us put up with basal readers that contain simple sentences, 99 percent of which began with a subject and really ended with a verb and then perhaps some kind of complement. Now, as we begin our writing careers either completing essays and term papers or dashing off a letter to a friend—even composing a newspaper article—grabbing the attention of the reader becomes essential; therefore, sentence variety needs emphasis.

Simply put, *sentence variety* means using a pattern different from subject-verb-complement (direct object or predicate noun). What are the possibilities?

1. Instead of a simple sentence use a complex, compound, or compound-complex sentence (see Chapter 7).

2. Begin the sentence with a prepositional phrase or a series of prepositional phrases. *In the middle of the physical workout with the new client*, Ron Alterio was called to the front desk. (three prepositional phrases at the beginning of the sentence)

3. Start a sentence with a direct object: *Misfortune* Daniel considered his lot.

4. Begin with a participial phrase: While starting his car the other morning, Mike Mariano discovered a crack in his windshield. (Just make sure that the phrase doesn't dangle.)

5. Use a gerund phrase or a noun clause as the subject.

   Straining to complete her strenuous exercise caused Wendy Keyes to swear audibly. (gerund phrase used as the subject)
   That many poems of Emily Dickinson appear cryptic cause many students to shun her writing. (noun clause as the subject)

6. Start the sentence with a single adjective and adverb.

ADVERB: _Unobtrusively_, Bill Sybert picked up his opponent's ball on the third green.

ADJECTIVE: _Unabashed_, Archie Erskine strode into the clubhouse after shooting another 110 on the Madison Country Club.

7. Use an adverb clause at the beginning of the sentence: _When Frank at the Madison Winter Club presents his annual roast duck dinner_, members scramble for tickets.

8. Start with an infinitive phrase: _To make it easier to attend Daytona events,_ Dave and Mildred Hoffman moved to Port Orange, the city next to Daytona.

9. Begin the sentence with two adverbs; also, begin the sentence with a pair of adjectives.

ADVERBS: _Calmly_ but _cautiously_, my cat Cassidy approached the chattering squirrel in anticipation of an unexpected dinner.

ADJECTIVES: _Stubborn_ and _brash_, Donna and Kathy refuse to quit smoking.

10. After writing a paragraph, look at the sentences and see what can be revised or what should stay. The care you begin your writing with leads to style. (see Chapter 17).

Task 30
Write a well-thought-out sentence according to the instructions below.
(Suggested answers appear on pages 183–184.)

1. Write a simple sentence.

2. Write a compound sentence.

3. Write a complex sentence.

4. Write a compound-complex sentence.

5. Write a sentence beginning with a prepositional phrase.

6. Write a sentence beginning with several prepositional phrases.

7. Write a sentence beginning with a direct object.

8. Write a sentence beginning with a participial phrase.

9. Write a sentence with a gerund phrase as the subject.

10. Write a sentence with a noun clause as the subject.

11. Write a sentence beginning with a single adjective.

12. Write a sentence beginning with two adjectives separated by a coordinating conjunction.

13. Write a sentence beginning with a single adverb.

14. Write a sentence beginning with two adverbs joined by a coordinating conjunction.

15. Write a sentence beginning with an adverb clause.

16. Write a sentence beginning with an infinitive phrase.

17. Write a paragraph (or two or three or more) that shows sentence variety.

14

Cumulative Review
Test of Chapters 2–13

If any of the sentences that follow are correct, place an "A" next to the number on your paper. If the sentence contains an error (or errors), identify the error by the letters B–L; then, rewrite the sentence correctly. Answers are on pages 184–185.

A—Correct sentence
B—Misplaced or dangling modifier
C—Incorrect coordination or subordination
D—Lack of parallel structure
E—Lack of agreement, subject and verb
F—Lack of agreement, pronoun and antecedent
G—Reference of pronoun error (GI—ambiguous, GII—indefinite, GIII—weak, GIV—general)
H—Incorrect tense or mood
I—Wrong case used
J—Passive voice needs to be changed to active voice
K—Fragment
L—Run-on

1. Michael James Rode was told by the administration of Georgetown that he had been selected to the college's Board of Trustees.

2. Amy Jirsa graduated from the University of Nebraska, acted on Broadway in three one-act plays, and then she went to Chicago to study the harp.

3. In the month of May, Bill Alberino suspended his teaching of *Macbeth*, and started *The Merchant of Venice* instead.

4. Joan Teri Rode was chosen not only as the girl most likely to succeed but also as the one least likely to take a bribe.

5. On June 11, 2001, Timothy McVeigh died by lethal injection he thought he might be granted a stay of execution but was denied.

6. Priscilla Rich, along with several of her closest friends, especially Nancy, Joan, and Cynthia, ride to Newark every other Thursday.

7. Clay Rich told his former boss that he was going to drive him crazy.

8. When Mr. McKiernan demanded that Andy Bakoledis is quiet, his girlfriend chastised the teacher for picking on the love of her life.

9. After rummaging around in the attic, Betty O'Shea found thirty-five pairs of shoes she had never worn.

10. If everyone gave up smoking, they would be better off.

11. To show absurdity at its utmost, Nancy Bennett was taken to the police station by an officer for fingerprinting and photographing mug shots—all because there was a warrant for her arrest for letting a dog roam.

12. Young Larry O'Shea, whom many people thought would be the next Clarence Darrow, fooled everyone and joined the circus.

13. Old Larry O'Shea cut the lawn twice on Thursday, which was all right with his boss.

14. Although Margaret Clark MacGruer thought that all the preparations for her husband's birthday party had been accomplished.

15. Ryan Dolan went to the carnival for excitement but there were none.

16. On one fishing trip Dewey Zuroweste caught his thumb in a reel, dropped four rigs overboard, and finished the day by cutting his foot on a broken beer bottle.

17. David Taylor MacKay, John Andrews, and Jack Andrews fish for lobsters; however, when the lobsters do not cooperate, they try for winkles instead.

18. Jogging near the bridge at Fence Creek, a snake suddenly darted from the side of the road and frightened Kathleen Sullivan.

19. When Erin Sullivan was an eighth grader, she was chosen both as a hall monitor and served as chief board eraser.

20. When Kathy G. Dolan told her teacher that she would have a good time in Budapest, she said that she would be there only three days.

21. Charles R. Daricek, the Fire Chief in Madison, recruits volunteers by newspaper advertisements in one week twenty men and fourteen women showed up for interviews.

22. Tony Milano has worked as a court stenographer and as a meat cutter, but in Branford he is known as "King Crab," because of the number of crustaceans he pulls out of the Branford River.

23. Paul Haye gave my wife and I an anniversary present, a trip to Sorrento, Italy.

24. It said on the cigarette carton that smoking could be dangerous to one's health.

25. Either Michelle or Judy Daricek threw the party for their mother, but since they're twins, no one knew for sure.

Manual of Usage

Usage today does not resemble usage of yesterday. Listen to television announcers mix up "bring" and "take" or hear at the bowling alley a disgruntled teammate saying, "It should have *went!* (referring to the pin still wobbling but still standing). Sunday during pro football season one would hear "These *kind* of running back . . ." and cringe because *this kind* or *these kinds* is the proper form. In his early days, Don Imus consistently mixed up *imply* and *infer*, but now he takes great pains with precise language.

What follows is appropriate for any situation: a *Times* editorial, a college essay, a talk in front of the Rotary, informal conversation, and even e-mail. True, there are levels of language where anything goes, but for the most part, words like *less* and *fewer*, *except* or *accept* should not be confused. At the risk of repeating the words of E. B. White in *Elements of Style*, or in Warriner's grammar and composition texts, or in *Fowler's*, or in any other usage manual, here goes:

A, an (indefinite article), *the* (definite article)

I was taught early on to use "an" before a vowel and when I had written "an union" on a paper in my freshman year, the teacher corrected it noting: Use "an" before a vowel *sound* (the teacher's emphasis) and "a" before a consonant sound. The one exception to this rule is with an "h" in "historical": Since the first syllable of "historical" is not stressed, "an" is used with it: "an" historical event.

Even "the" changes before a vowel sound, but only in pronunciation. Before vowel sounds, "the" sounds like "thee" but before consonant sounds "the" sounds like "thuh." "A" or "an" with a noun can mean any, as in a rifle; "the" designates particular as in the Winchester.

Accept, except

The word "accept" means to receive and is a verb; "except" in most cases is a preposition meaning with the exclusion or exception of but can also be a verb meaning to take or leave out from a number or a whole.

Frank Ford, the day manager at O'Farrel's on 33rd Street, accepted (verb) the New York State Bartender of the Year Award.

Every bartender in Key West was present at the ceremonies except (preposition) Leigh, whose boss at the Schooner Galley would not let her off.

Because the teacher excepted (verb) my lowest three grades, I passed English for the semester.

Affect, effect

Mostly a verb, "affect" (to influence, to impress, to sway); mostly a noun, "effect" (the result, the accomplishment, the intent, and yes, even the influence). What confuses everyone then? "Affect" can be a noun (the conscious subjective aspect of an emotion considered apart from bodily changes), but only one studying psychology, perhaps, would consider using "affect" in this sense (and put the accent on the first syllable). "Effect" can be a verb (to cause to happen, to accomplish, to bring about).

Alcohol affects (verb meaning influences) the way one thinks.

What effect (noun meaning result, influence) did the designated hitter have on the game of baseball?

When the Board of Education effected (verb meaning caused, brought about) the change in vacations, the faculty protested with a strike.

Ain't

Fowler's: ". . . it leads a shadowy existence. . . . It stands, as it were, at the door, out on the pavement, not yet part of any standard paradigm in the drawing-room." The educated or streetwise know when and when not to use "ain't."

Allusion, illusion

Almost always "to" follows "allusion" (an implied or indirect reference especially in literature); similarly, "of" many times follows "illusion" (something that deceives or misleads intellectually).

Shakespeare's allusions to religious practices baffle many readers.

Astounding audiences everywhere, Harry Houdini once created an illusion of an elephant disappearing.

Alright, all right

It's not all right to use "alright." Enough said.

Already, all ready

The first, an adverb meaning previously or prior to; the second, a group prepared.

Without his glasses, Pete Weiss had <u>already</u> shot the "wild turkey" but suddenly realized it was the neighbor's dog he had done in.

Peter and Eric Weiss were <u>all ready</u> to fly to Bermuda, but Bradley Airport in Hartford was closed.

Alumna, alumnae, alumnus, alumni

(See Appendix 4 for an anecdote about the use of the word "alumnus.")

alumna—one female graduate: Erin, my youngest daughter, is an <u>alumna</u> of Providence College.

alumnae—more than one female graduate: Shauna, my middle daughter, and Erin are <u>alumnae</u> of Providence College.

alumnus—one male graduate: Dr. Dan Fitzgerald is an <u>alumnus</u> of Providence College.

alumni—more than one male graduate or more than one male and female graduate: Dr. Richard Landino, Dr. Mark Catania, and Dr. Bob Gallo are all <u>alumni</u> of Providence College.

Among, between

Use "between" for two items; use "among" for three or more.

Ernst J. King spends his gambling time <u>between</u> Foxwoods and Mohegan Sun.

Helen Veronica Lipp divided her sweepstakes winnings <u>among</u> ten of her closest friends.

But: John Henry Miller Jr., a collector of rare antiques from the Elizabethan Era, shares his expertise (<u>between, among</u>) several dealers in New England. (Here you would choose "between" because John Henry deals separately with each dealer. The dealers are considered as individuals.)

Amount, number

If items are counted or plural, use "number" in almost all cases; if an item is quantitative, or one unit, or singular, use "amount" in most cases.

Nancy Bennet had a <u>number</u> of issues she had to deal with when she went for her sons' parent conferences. ("Issues" is plural; therefore, "number" is used.)

The DEP dealt quickly with the huge <u>amount</u> of snow this winter. ("Snow" is singular; therefore, "amount" is used.)

But: I could not count the <u>number</u> of snowflakes that fell in one hour.

And etc.

Redundancy at its best. Since "et cetera" means "and so on," there is no necessity in repeating "and"; "etc." will do.

At (after "where")

"Where is the library <u>at</u>?" rankles grammarians twofold: First, one never (or almost never) ends a sentence with a preposition; second, "at" and "where" are redundant.

Because, reason

Never use "because" after the word "reason" as in: The <u>reason</u> the Yankees won the pennant three times in a row was <u>because</u> the front office could buy any player available. ("Reason" and "because" are redundant.) Change this sentence in three ways:

"The Yankees won the pennant <u>because</u> . . ."
". . . was <u>that</u> the front office . . ."
". . . row was the front office . . ."

Beside, besides

"Beside" means next to and "besides" means in addition to. There's not much chance of mixing up these two.

Bring, take

These two words appear on almost every SAT test of writing skills. "Bring" is used when the action is coming toward the speaker, but "take" implies action going away from the speaker. That formula will work ninety percent of the time, but what is the choice in the following:

When we go to watch Harvard play Yale in Yale Bowl, we should <u>(bring, take)</u> pillows for the rock-hard seats. I'd say "take" because of the word "go," but have argued with those who choose "bring."

When Jeff Shepherd bought Witt's End Pub in the center of Guilford, he hoped to <u>bring</u> many customers with him. (Though not technically the speaker, the action is coming toward Jeff.)

Quippy <u>takes</u> his cell phone even when he goes to work on the *Half Shell*, a clam dredger out of Milford, Connecticut. ("Going" is stated here.)

Compliment, complement

The first is what we all crave, formal recognition or a pat on the back; the second is something that fills up or completes (like the predicate noun or predicate adjective).

Dr. Bill McCullough and his wife Barbara always <u>compliment</u> Dan and Nancy when the latter couple serves at parties.

Richie Hahn has nothing but <u>compliments</u> for the fire chief and the police chief: He thinks they can do nothing wrong.

My wife complements me: She knows all there is to know, and I know all the rest.

The beige jacket worn by Izzy Hahn complemented the new shoes she had just bought at Lord and Taylor.

Creditable (praiseworthy), *credible* (believable), *credulous* (easily believing, gullible), *incredible* (beyond belief), *incredulous* (skeptical)

Ron Freytag said that I usually did a creditable job in setting him up for the night shift.

The story the young man told seemed credible, but there were parts of it that defied truth.

Ben Kupcho convinced the credulous student that the Pentagon had eight sides.

David Copperfield performs some incredible feats, like making a plane disappear.

Incredulous of the doctor's pronouncement of twins, the young mother said that multiple births had never been part of her family history.

Data, phenomena, strata, loci, stadia, genii, criteria, and *media,* are plural for the following: *datum, phenomenon, stratum, locus, stadium, genie, criterion,* and *medium.* Therefore, the first group takes plural verbs, and the second group takes singular verbs.

Professor Elizabeth Hahn told her future English teachers that all the data they needed for their projects were available in the Southern Connecticut Library.

Richard Hahn's criteria for working include punctuality, diligence, and complete obedience to the boss.

Tony Milano once said that the media are responsible for ruining the crab population in the Branford River.

Discover, invent

Not too much of a problem, but worth noting: To discover something means that the something already exists. When one invents an item, that item is just "born."

In 1751 Axel Frederik Cronstedt discovered nickel. (Nickel was waiting for someone to find it.)

In 1816 Rene Theophile Hyacinthe Laennec invented the stethoscope. (Obviously Laennec did not trip over it.)

Double negative

"If Shakespeare can use the double negative, I can use it too." But: "The double negative proves only that the person using it is uneducated." Somewhere between lies the truth. Catch this exchange between the two gentlemen from Verona from, of course, *Two Gentlemen of Verona*:

Proteus: Over the boots? <u>Nay</u>, give me <u>not</u> the boots.
Valentine: <u>No</u>, I will <u>not</u>; for it boots thee <u>not</u>.

If you ask a friend for some money, and he answers with: "I ain't got none," would there be any problem with what he said? Unequivocally, he has no money. However, what he is really saying is: "I have some money, but you're not getting any" (two negatives making a positive). There still is no problem because you know he's broke, you know what he means, and you know you're not getting the money.

Using double negatives today sometimes indicates a lack of refinement, possibly a lack of education. Also, double negatives seem to occur in informal speech rather than in college essays or in formal dissertations. I think that if one can be objective about double negatives, he has solved the problem.

Here, then is a list of obvious negative words that should be used sparingly: not, never, none, and no. (Never use "ain't" unless the character one writes about talks that way.) Not so obvious negatives are: only and but.

I <u>ain't never</u> seen such pomposity. (Actually I'd like to meet this person who uses a double negative *and* the word "pomposity" in the same breath.) *Should be:* I have <u>never</u> seen such pomposity.
I have <u>not but</u> one choice. *Should be:* I have <u>only</u> one choice.

And there are expressions that are creeping into the language, but still are considered negative:

I could<u>n't</u> help <u>but</u> think badly about Joe.

Instead of trying to emulate Shakespeare or fooling others into thinking you're not too swift, be yourself and avoid the use of double negatives—be positive or use just one negative at a time.

Either . . . or, neither . . . nor

Never mix these up:

Rachael Shavaughn <u>neither</u> lost her pocketbook <u>or</u> lost her ticket to Bermuda. (Once using "neither," you must continue with "nor.")

Therefore: Rachael Shavaughn <u>neither</u> lost her pocketbook <u>nor</u> lost her ticket to Bermuda.

Emigrate, immigrate

If, like my mother-in-law, Annie Shehan, when she was eighteen in 1906, a person leaves a country (Ireland) to settle in another country (America), she emigrates. If the emphasis changes and the person comes into a country, she immigrates. An emigrant leaves but an immigrant comes into. An émigré is a person forced out of a country for political reasons.

Fewer, less

Use the first one ("fewer") with a plural noun and the second ("less") with a singular noun.

On opening day 2001, the Mets had <u>fewer</u> (because the noun it goes with is plural) fans than did the Yankees.

When my neighbor planted a huge vegetable garden, she had <u>less</u> (because the word it goes with is singular in form, even though it designates many blades) grass to mow.

Imply, infer

Possibly the most important words to know while you're being tested on reading comprehension: "What does the author <u>imply</u> in Paragraph 2?" Or, "What should the reader <u>infer</u> from the first sentence of Paragraph 4?" These questions are usually followed by five choices, one of which is a literal meaning of the answer, not what is hinted at or what is to be deduced. Tricky, aren't they?

Imply, implied, implying, implication, implicit

All these forms of "imply" contain the idea of suggestion, hint, and indirectness rather than the literal; they also suggest speaker, writer, or actor, all of whom by words or actions can imply to the inside.

Infer, inference, inferring, inferential

These words contain ideas of deduction, concluding, the gathering of facts to draw a conclusion; these words also suggest listener, reader, or audience, those who are inferring.

When my economics teacher told us to put in extra hours of study, we <u>inferred</u> that the test would be a killer.

But: When my economics teacher told us to put in extra hours of study, she <u>implied</u> the test would be a killer.

To distinguish between "imply" and "infer," determine the origin of the action and you will rarely be in doubt.

The ticket clerk at Aer Lingus <u>implied</u> that there would be a strike tomorrow when she said that we should change our flight plans. (She hinted or suggested there would be a strike, but she did not say it.)

The tourists <u>inferred</u> traffic lights meant nothing in Naples, Italy when they witnessed several vehicles speeding through the red. (Watching cars and trucks go through red lights, the tourists put two and two together.)

In, into

"In" should be used to mean within. "Into" implies going from the outside.

CORRECT: When Isolyn Ying O'Brien went <u>into</u> the walk-in freezer, she found several packages of hamburger buns dated 1999.

CORRECT: Charles Dwight Loveland found a huge moth <u>in</u> his closet.

INCORRECT: Emily C. Zimmermann dove <u>in</u> the pool. (This sentence might be correct, however, if indeed Emily were *in* the pool and diving, but chances are she was on the side of the pool or on a board and dived into the pool.)

It's, its

The confusion occurs because of the possessive, "its." When we use a noun and make it possessive, we add an apostrophe—as in *the lance's point* or *Russell's desk*. It would also follow then that we would add an apostrophe to "it" when "it" is used in the possessive. But the apostrophe is removed when "it" is possessive. Thus, <u>its</u> form, <u>its</u> radiance, <u>its</u> over-all beauty makes the rose the symbol of love.

"It's," on the other hand, means it is. The "i" is missing and needs the apostrophe to take its place. Enough said.

Emily Dickinson had fun with "it's." She used "it's" for both the contraction and the possessive. For example, in Poem # 383, in the last stanza she speaks of a train engine in terms of a horse:

And neigh like Boanerges—
Then—prompter than a Star—
Stop—docile and omnipotent
At **it's** own stable door—

Lay, lie

Consistently confused. Learn the parts first, then the meanings:

lay, laid, laid, laying—to put or set down; to place for rest or sleep

lie, lay, lain, lying—to assume a horizontal position; to be prostrate; to rest or to recline

E. B. White's explanation of "lay": "The hen, or the play, <u>lays</u> an egg." The rest of the examples are mine:

Lying down after a hard day raking leaves, I restore my energy enough to surf the web.

Laying the baby in the crib, the young mother breathed a sigh of relief.

Lazarus <u>had lain</u> in the tomb for four days but sprang to life after Jesus' Word.

But: The sister and wife <u>had laid</u> Lazarus in the tomb, and when Jesus told other relatives to remove the stone, the crowd thought His words to be a hoax.

Notice that "lay" can take an object (but not always); "lie" cannot take an object.

Like, as, as if

If you can remember that "like" is a preposition and introduces a phrase, no error will occur. Also, the other two, "as" and "as if" introduce a clause.

Jan Dephouse drove the first tee <u>like Tiger Woods</u> but three putted for a double bogie. (phrase underlined)

Butch Cooney ate the cashews on the bar <u>as if he had starved himself for three days.</u> (clause underlined)

Kind, sort, type (with "this," "that," "these," "those")

"This" and "that" are singular; therefore, they must accompany "kind," "sort," and "type." "These" and "those" are plural and go with "kinds," "sorts," and "types." Egregious error: "These kind" or "those sort." One would hardly say "this kinds" or "that sorts."

For perfect decoration, <u>these kinds</u> of flowers are necessary.

<u>This kind</u> of pen will last for three years of constant use.

Ray Dudley will not put up with <u>this sort</u> of behavior.

I cannot write unless I use <u>this type</u> of bond paper.

Kind of, sort of

Do not use these expressions to mean somewhat or rather.

POOR: Edwin Oswaldo Sarmiento Lituma didn't fish because it was <u>sort of</u> foggy.

BETTER: Edwin Oswaldo Sarmiento Lituma didn't fish because it was <u>some-what</u> foggy.

POOR: I declined the movie invitation because I was <u>kind of</u> tired.

BETTER: I declined the movie invitation because I was <u>rather</u> tired.

kinda, sorta—Just do not ever use!

Kind of a, sort of a, type of a

The "a" is not needed.
WRONG: Most students prefer that <u>kind of a</u> notebook.
CORRECT: Most students prefer that <u>kind of</u> notebook.

Nauseous, nauseated

"I feel <u>nauseous</u>." To say this statement means that you have a detrimental effect on those around you because you cause disgust. Although this situation might be true, what should be said is "I feel <u>nauseated</u>" because a sickness of some kind is about to ruin the day. "Nauseous" means disgusting, but "nauseated" means sick. That was then. Now, *Webster's Collegiate* states: "Current evidence shows these facts: *nauseous* is most frequently used to mean physically affected with nausea, usu. after a linking verb such as *feel* or *become*; figurative use is quite a bit less frequent. Use of *nauseous* in sense 1 [causing nausea or disgust] is much more often figurative than literal, and this use appears to be losing ground to *nauseating. Nauseated,* while not rare, is less common than *nauseous* in sense 2 [affected with nausea or disgust]."

Off of

The "of" in this construction is implied by "off" and therefore is superfluous. Using "from" usually settles the matter, but with trains, busses, boats, bicycles, and planes a different matter arises because a person gets "off" them whereas the same person gets "out of" a car. Jumping "from" any of these modes of transportation implies danger.

WRONG: Jonathan Mulvey jumped <u>off of</u> the snowy ledge.
BETTER: Gregory Mulvey jumped <u>off</u> the snowy ledge.
BEST: Matthew Mulvey jumped <u>from</u> the snowy ledge.

Respectively, respectfully

The first, "respectively," means each in the order presented. The second word, "respectfully," means full of respect and admiration.

Lenny Wilkens played at Boys' High in Brooklyn, at Providence College, for the St. Louis Hawks, and for the Seattle Super Sonics in 1955, 1959, 1963, and 1969, <u>respectively</u>.
Mary Kelley Maloney <u>respectfully</u> turned in her resignation.

Should of, would of, could of, might of, must of

These terms have appeared in our language because of the pronunciation of the correct terms: should've, would've, could've, might've, must've. Therefore, in a formal paper or essay or answer to a test question, if we do not abbreviate, this problem is already solved with "should have," "would have," "could have," "might have," and "must have." "Shoulda," "woulda," "coulda," "mighta," and "musta" are out of the question.

So

In standard written English and in formal speech, "so" is not to be used by itself. Why do you think babies become confused when we raise our arms in front of them and say, "So big!"? The little ones are saying to themselves, "These dudes know not their grammar."

Use "so" with "that":

Missy Frey volunteered for the language arts steering committee <u>so that</u> the English Department would dictate the curriculum.

Eric Weiss decided to fly for Spirit Airlines <u>so that</u> he could acquire buddy passes for his friends.

Noel Slatter Heimer was <u>so</u> frustrated with the students in the library <u>that</u> she kept the entire class after school.

<u>So</u> fervent was Jan Dephouse in playing golf <u>that</u> he enrolled in the Pete Boswell School of Duffers.

In informal speech or conversation, "so" can be used by itself:

I am <u>so</u> tired.

Mets season tickets went on sale, <u>so</u> Bill Breck headed toward Shea Stadium.

Some, somewhat, rather

Never use "some" to mean somewhat or rather as in

That pie was <u>some</u> good.

MUCH BETTER: That pie was <u>rather</u> good.

BUT: I had <u>some</u> time at the dance. (Here, "some" seems to mean more than somewhat or rather, which would not fit any way.)

Than, then

These words are mixed up because, when pronounced quickly, they sound alike. "Than" is a comparison word, however, and "then" designates a past or future time.

Cynthia Ruth Cole has read more Shakespeare <u>than</u> any other student in her class.

Mark Petronio attended a Celtics game in the afternoon; <u>then</u>, he decided to fly to New York to see the Patriots play the Jets.

That was <u>then</u>; this is now.

That, which, who

Use "who" (or "whom") when referring to persons, "which" to refer to inanimate objects and animals (all those things not persons), and "that" to refer to both; however, Mark Twain said that he suspected bad things about writers who used "that" to refer to a human being.

Larry Wardlaw, <u>who</u> owned an oil business in Branford, Connecticut, thinks the Knicks are mediocre at best.

The album <u>that</u> Leo Bruyette loves best is "The Best of Irish Ballads."

Their, they're, there

Perhaps the problem here occurs because each of these begins with "the-." But mixing them up has caused much consternation among instructors. To avoid trouble, learn them.

<u>Their</u> confidence makes Dwayne Wade and Nate Robinson excellent players.

<u>They're</u> the best they can be.

<u>There</u> is where we should go.

Type of a, sort of a, kind of a

The "a" is superfluous.

<u>This type</u> of scenery . . .
<u>This sort</u> of movie . . .   <u>*All*</u> without the **a**.
<u>This kind</u> of cookie . . .

Way, ways

Use "way" to mean distance, not "ways."

Arthur Jerome Finnerty drove a long <u>way</u> (not "ways") to visit his relatives.

Rio is a long <u>way</u> (not "ways") from here.

But (with apology to Paul Simon): How many <u>ways</u> are there to leave a lover?

Here, "ways" means modes or manners.

Where, when

These words are not to be used in a definition.

An ace is <u>when</u> the server in tennis serves a ball that is not returned.

A bogie occurs <u>when</u> a golfer shoots one over par on a given hole.

A technical knockout (TKO) in a prizefight is <u>where</u> the referee decides that one fighter cannot continue.

A picaresque novel is <u>where</u> the main character experiences several different events in several different places.

These types of errors should be eliminated by revising the entire sentence. Just leaving the incorrect words out will not suffice.

An ace in tennis is a serve not returned by an opponent.

A bogie in golf is one over par on a given hole.

A technical knockout (TKO) in a prizefight occurs if the referee decides that one fighter cannot continue.

In a picaresque novel, the main character experiences several different events in several different places.

But in the following sentence, <u>where</u> and <u>when</u> are used correctly because the sentence is not a definition of anything:

June 27, 2002, in Cromwell, Connecticut, was <u>when</u> and <u>where</u> Wally Camp was inducted into the High School Athletic Directors Hall of Fame.

Who, whom; whoever, whomever

These two pairs of words might be mixed up more than any other pair. The problem might be because the person speaking or writing does not know the difference between "objective" or "subjective." Otherwise, an explanation is simple: "Who" is subjective; that is, "who" is used only as a subject or a predicate pronoun. Consider the following examples:

Ralph Garcia, <u>who</u> speaks Spanish and English fluently, can also get along in both Italian and French. (Subject of the adjective clause)

The person most responsible for the New York Stock Exchange's success is <u>who</u>? (Predicate pronoun)

"Whom" is objective; that is, "whom" is used as an object of the preposition or direct object—but never as a subject or predicate pronoun.

Harold "Boomer" Eddy, to <u>whom</u> the City of Wallingford bestowed the honor of "Our Best Baseballer," taught math in Durham for thirty-eight years. ("Whom" is the object of "to.")

<u>Whom</u> do you like in the next Presidential election? ("Whom" is the direct object of "do like.")

"Whoever" and "whomever" follow the same rules as "who" and "whom": "whoever" is subjective and "whomever" is objective. However, "whoever" is always the subject of a clause; "whomever" is always the object:

The Yale Club Award is presented to [<u>whoever</u> does the most for the welfare of scholars in America.] ("Whoever" is the subject of the clause; even though the word "to" appears next to "whoever," it is the clause itself that serves as the direct object, not the word "whoever.") Chip and Joan Stone invited [<u>whomever</u> they deemed their close friends]; a thousand guests showed up. ("Whomever" is in the objective case, the clause itself is the object of "invited," and the subject of the clause is "they.")

USAGE TEST

Some of the following sentences contain errors in usage. Next to the number of the correct sentences, write "C." Next to the numbers of sentences with usage errors, rewrite the sentence or correct the usage error. (Answers are on pages 185–186.)

1. If Shelly Tolles had not brought his "Benny Hill" tape to the Dolly, the altercation never would have occurred.

2. Dick Shuler said that there are an inordinate amount of Chinese restaurants in New York City.

3. When Thelma E. Johnson stated that she hated gambling, she inferred that Las Vegas was not a good vacation spot.

4. How the graffiti on the walls of the school effected Dana Michael Valeriay no one will ever know.

5. Peg and Bill Robertson had to decide between a Cadillac and a Pontiac for their prize, but instead they opted for cash.

6. Instead of going to Maine for that weekend of horrible weather, Lorrie S. Johnson thought that she and her family should of stayed home.

7. Stanley M. Johnson decided that less mudslides per week would be better for him.

8. When she left for Los Angeles, Jean Tolles forgot to bring her crossword puzzles and had nothing to keep her occupied during the flight.

9. When Jen Landon read her acceptance letter from the School of Theater at New York University, she jumped up and down for joy.

10. The reason Elizabeth DeBurra Valeriay joined the March for Autism is because she teaches handicapped youngsters in Fairfield.

11. Last year, Ireland exported less lambs than the year before because of the foot and mouth threat.

12. Like he had done for several years, Dana Michael Valeriay took his Harley to Daytona for Race Week.

13. At the anniversary party, Sean Matthew Landon consumed an amazing amount of jelly donuts from the Hometown Bakery.

14. During our conversation, Luis Abarco made an illusion to the number of cats he owns.

15. Even though Joseph William Cooper Jr. said that he felt alright, his mother decided he should stay home from school.

16. Beside serving on the Parents' Board at Our Lady of Mercy School, Erin Tiernan Cooper also coached the girls' basketball team.

17. When Joseph William Cooper Sr. walked in the auditorium, he noticed that his picture had been placed on the wall.

18. Just before dinner, Joseph Fallon Cooper complained of a headache and thought he might go lay down.

19. An outstanding student in both high school and college, Kerry Elizabeth Fasano accepted a position with a prestigious trading firm.

20. Because she had seen me twice bartending at Malone's, Erin Fasano inferred that I worked there full time.

21. The reason the band at Daniel Hand High School rates as number one in New England is because Richard Fasano, the band director, insists on perfection.

22. Ryan Fasano effected the change in the sports program at High Hill School when he introduced fencing into the curriculum.

23. Sandy Beach Newberg thought that that kind of a car belonged in a museum.

24. "A Texas League single," said Richard Barry, "is when a ball hit just over the infielders' heads and drops in front of the outfielders."

25. Sean Barry could not except the town engineer saying that the area near Buffalo Bay would become a shopping mall.

Writing the Paragraph

So far, most of the emphasis has centered on words, phrases, clauses, and sentences; however, usually what the student has to face and perhaps what we remember most from formal schooling looms up in reality and in memory as *the essay*. Writing the perfect essay assumes perfect paragraphing; perfect paragraphing assumes knowledge of words, phrases, clauses, and sentences, and, of course, something poignant to say.

Topic Sentence

Teachers hammer away at the topic sentence, the be-all and the end-all of all paragraphs. "The topic sentence must come at the beginning of the paragraph," one teacher told the class, but one youngster did not buy the dictum: "My father says that the topic sentence may appear at the beginning, middle, or end of the paragraph!" The student received a detention for his brashness, but subsequently the teacher found out that for twenty-five years the father had taught Advanced Writing at the local university. Apologizing profusely, the teacher had learned a quick lesson in writing.

THE TOPIC SENTENCE AT THE BEGINNING

We start, then, with the premise that the topic sentence does not necessarily come first, although statistically, one might say, that many times it does. Check the following paragraph with the topic sentence underlined:

The life of a wise man is most of all extemporaneous, for he lives out of an eternity which includes all time. The cunning mind travels further back than Zoroaster each instant, and comes quite down to the present with its revelation. The utmost thrift and industry of thinking give no man any stock in life; his credit with the inner world is no better, his capital no larger. He must try his fortune again to-day [sic] as yesterday. All questions rely on the present for their solution. Time measures nothing but itself. The word that is written may be postponed, but not that on the lip. If this is what the occasion says, let the occasion say it. All the world is forward to prompt him who gets up to live without his creed in his pocket.

(from *A Week on the Concord and Merrimack Rivers,* "Thursday," by Henry David Thoreau)

For the neophyte writer, the beginning topic sentence steers the direction of thought. Also, placing the topic sentence first helps the essay writer faced with the daunting task of filling a bluebook with the response to a question. "Start your essay by recasting the question so that the essence of the question is the substance of your topic sentence," echoes in colleges every time an essay is required. Learning this dictum from high school may be the best piece of advice you ever receive. Look at the following example.

QUESTION: Why did Ralph Waldo Emerson leave the ministry?
ANSWER: Ralph Waldo Emerson left the ministry because . . .

THE CLINCHER

Practicing writing paragraphs broadens the scope of the writer and gives the writing variety. Long paragraphs, especially, need what many call the *clincher*, the sentence at the end that reminds the reader (and the writer, for that matter) what the paragraph is about. The clincher repeats the idea of the first sentence in the paragraph, but states it in different words.

In the following paragraph from *The Elements of Style* by William Strunk Jr. and E. B. White, notice how the *idea* is repeated but in different words:

Youth invariably speaks to youth in a tongue of his own devising: he renovates the language with a wild vigor, as he would a basement apartment. By the time this paragraph sees print, *uptight, ripoff, rap, dude, vibes, copout,* and *funky* will be the words of yesteryear, and we will be fielding more recent ones that have come bouncing into our speech—some of them into our dictionary as well. A new word is always up for survival. Many do survive. Others grow stale and disappear. Most are, at least in their infancy, more appropriate to conversation than to composition.

TOPIC SENTENCE AT THE END

To vary the paragraph, some writers place the topic sentence at the end. This technique, although fairly uncommon, draws the reader to a conclusion by introducing a "list" of items that naturally enfold into a full picture. In the following paragraph, the author intends description and follows up with a topic sentence that includes all the preceding details.

A seagull dropped a clam on the rock nestled in the marsh while a hovering osprey was just tucking his wings, having spotted an unwary flounder in the shallows. A mother mallard guided her youngsters to the left bank where a meal waited where the bank mussels stood out gray in the low tide. Two terns squeaked by heading for the bay because there were no tidbits here. A turtle poked his head out of the water to say hello as we glided through the mirror of the river. <u>Nature never fails to entertain and amaze us at the beginning of every fishing trip.</u>

By Dan Mulvey

TOPIC SENTENCE AT THE BEGINNING AND END

This next one is a paragraph I wrote for a magazine that now does not exist. It was supposed to be a paragraph describing "My Fishing Buddy." I decided that the topic sentence should occur both at the beginning and end of the paragraph, the one at the end reminding the reader what it was about.

<u>My fishing buddy is generous to a fault</u>, but his wallet is strangely empty when we pull up to the gas dock. He will call at all hours of the morning, usually when you and everyone else in the house are still asleep, to say that he will be able to fish tomorrow, which is really today, according to the clock. Once at 11:30 one morning, as we were smack dab in the middle of an acre of bluefish chasing bunker, he announced that he had a noon appointment and that we should leave now! He will cater one trip with food fit for a French king, but the next time bring sandwiches and beer that have been around awhile. He knows everything about the type of fishing with which we are presently focused, but generally he is the one skunked, with no fish to lug home. <u>He is my fishing buddy.</u>

By Dan Mulvey

For the beginning writer, then, writing the paragraph starts with an idea, continues with the development of the topic sentence, and ends with the finished product. These are the other considerations:

- What type of paragraph is needed?

- How must the details be arranged?

- Is there transition between (and among) the sentences?

- Is the final product unified and coherent?

Task

Using the suggested words, write a topic sentence. (No answers are given.)

1. Diplomacy

2. Writing

3. Travel

4. Computers

5. Honesty

6. Snow

7. Fog

8. Dieting

9. Secrets

10. Fishing

Now write a paragraph using the topic sentence you have written. If the topic sentence does not seem to fit, write it again.

Types of Paragraphs

Writing the paragraph has baffled students and teachers alike, but to set down hard and fast rules further complicates the matter. How long should the paragraph be? Is there enough transition to clear the thought and help the reader? If the first paragraph is long, should I make the second one shorter? Longer? Have I said what I wanted to say?

These questions and more make writing the paragraph as individual as batting stances in the Major Leagues. From sentence paragraphs in the *Times* to the book length paragraph in Marquez's *The Autumn of the Patriarch,* most "normal" paragraphs comprise three to twelve sentences, sometimes more, sometimes fewer. Therefore, how long a paragraph should be rests with the author.

Even categorizing paragraphs borders on the dangerous, but keep in mind, these are suggestions only. You the writer may develop a paragraph according to the following designs: anecdote or incident with a beginning middle and end, comparison, contrast, comparison-contrast, cause and effect, definition or description, facts, examples, argument, or a combination of some of the aforementioned; having a plan of writing, especially in an essay or essay-type test, gives you at least a start. Take a look at some examples from the experts.

This descriptive paragraph is from Edna O'Brien's *Down by the River*, page 123.

Smoke was rising from the town chimneys, different plumes, tapers at first, then getting fatter and fatter as they went up, then breaking apart, fragmenting into nothing. Nothing. In her schoolbag were her books and her diary. Yes, Tara would cry. There was a chatter to the water like scolding old women, then slipshod at the edges where it was being sucked in and drunk by the tubers and roots of the golden reeds. Somewhere on the street near where the fish that busied Luke would be playing, playing to the heedless people who went by and filled with that lamp-like evening exhilaration. Goodbye Luke. The river rushed and purled along as if it was expected somewhere, each new swathe of water following upon the preceding one to its destination. The sky which had been a blaze of resiny life a while before was paling now, wooly grey clouds, and very soon it would be dark.

Here is another descriptive paragraph from Russell Banks's collection of stories, *The Angel on the Roof,* page 45.

The bob-house is only as large as need be, six feet by four feet is enough, and six feet high for a normal-sized person. At one end is a door with a step-over sill to keep out the wind, and at the other a homemade woodstove. Along one of the long walls is a narrow bench that serves as a seat and also as a bed when you want to nap or sleep over the night. Your traps and lines are set up along the opposite wall. There is a small window opening, but it remains covered by a hinged, wooden panel, keeping the bob-house in total darkness. When no light enters the bob-house, you can sit inside and peer through the holes in the ice and see clearly the world below. You see what the fish see, and you see them, too. But they cannot see you. You see the muddy lake bottom, undulating weeds, and decaying leaves, and, in a cold, green light, you see small schools of bluegills drift over the weed beds in search of food and oxygen, and coming along behind them three or four pickerel glide into view, looking for stragglers. Here and there a batch of yellow perch cruise past, and slowly, sleepily, a black bass. The light filtered through the ice is still, hard, and cold, like an algebraic equation, and you can watch the world pass through it with a clarity, objectivity, and love that is usually thought to be the exclusive prerogative of gods.

A generic incident from Melville, *Moby Dick*, "Chapter 62, The Dart," follows. Notice the "no wonder . . ." parallel structure, the use of "that" to refer to a person, and the description of the harpooner as part of this incident.

According to the invariable usage of the fishery, the whale-boat pushes off from the ship, with the headsman or whale-killer as temporary steersman, and the harpooner or whale-fastener pulling the foremost oar, the one known as the harpooner-oar. Now it needs a strong, nervous arm to strike the first iron into the fish, for often, in what is called the long dart, the heavy implement has to be flung for the distance of twenty to thirty feet. But however prolonged and exhausting the chase, the harpooner is expected to pull his oar meanwhile to the uttermost; indeed, he is expected to set an example of superhuman activity to the rest, not only by incredible rowing, but by repeated loud and intrepid exclamations; and what it is to keep shouting at the top of one's compass, while all the other muscles are strained and half started—what that is none know but those who have tried it. For one, I cannot bawl very heartily and work very recklessly at one and the same time. In this straining, bawling state, then, with his back to the fish, all at once the exhausted harpooner hears the exciting cry—"Stand up, and give it to him!" He now has to drop and secure his oar, turn round on his center half way, seize his harpoon from the crotch, and with what little strength may remain, he essays to pitch it somehow into the whale. No wonder, taking the whole fleet of whalemen in a body, that out of fifty fair chances for a dart, not five are successful; no wonder that so many hapless harpooners are madly cursed and disrated; no wonder that some of them actually burst their blood-vessels in the boat; no wonder that some sperm whalemen are absent four years with four barrels; no wonder that to many ship owners, whaling is but a losing concern; for it is the harpooner that makes the voyage, and if you take the breath out of his body how can you expect to find it there when most wanted?

Next, read carefully the paragraph by Henry David Thoreau from *A Week on the Concord and Merrimack Rivers*, written in the first half of the nineteenth century.

Shad are still taken in the Basin of Concord River at Lowell, where they are said to be a month earlier than the Merrimack shad, on account of the warmth of the water. Still patiently, almost pathetically, with instinct not to be discouraged, not to be reasoned with, revisiting their old haunts, as if their stern fates would relent, and still met by the Corporation with its dam. Poor shad! Where is thy redress? When nature gave thee instinct, gave she thee the heart to bear thy fate? Still wandering the sea in thy scaly armor to inquire humbly at the mouth of rivers if man has perchance left them free for thee to enter. By countless shoals loitering uncertain meanwhile, merely stemming the tide there, in danger from sea foes in spite of thy bright armor, awaiting new instructions, until the sands, until the water itself, tell thee if it be so or not. Thus by whole migrating nations, full of instinct, which is thy faith, in this backward spring, turned adrift, and perchance knowest not where men do not dwell, where there are not factories, in these days. Armed with no sword, no electric shock, but mere Shad, armed only with innocence and a just cause, with tender dumb mouth only forward, and scales easily to be detached. I for one am with thee, and who knows what may avail a crow-bar against that Billerica dam?—Not despairing when whole myriads have gone to feed sea monsters during thy suspense, but still brave, indifferent, on easy fin there, like shad reserved for higher destinies. . . .

With shad personified, Thoreau presents to the reader in this long paragraph definition, contrast, facts, and examples. The vocabulary, although simple, puts forth lofty ideas about a New England phenomenon.

Here is a comparison paragraph written by a former student.

A waitress and an actress are housed far apart, one in the maze of tables and the other in the glare of footlights, but each night both must prepare to play a role. As the waitress ties on her apron and pins up her hair, an actress dons her costume and paints her face. The actress commits her lines and blocking to memory, knows when to roll her eyes, when to change the lilt of her voice, when to exit gracefully. A waitress's script is far less dramatic and artful but just as thoroughly rehearsed and delivered: Greet the guests smiling, converse charmingly while clearing away plates, crumbs, and glasses, then deliver the check graciously and discreetly. The waitress and the actress have an audience to please though the former's stage is limited to an eight by four table, but the waitress makes herself scarce and appears only on cue. Both, however, have their performances rated at the end of the evening. The generous audience stands and applauds one while the other "audience" leaves a healthy tip on the table. And when the curtain falls on night's end, the actress may sit among the hundreds of roses from adoring fans while the waitress feels the tight wad of bills in her apron pocket. Both are alone. The actress then removes her makeup, and the waitress sits laughing in the dark bend of the bar, hair and apron unleashed. Two different players leave their stages, their acts over until tomorrow night.

By Laura Marie Harrison, a former student of the author (used with permission of the author). At the time of the writing, Laura was about to enter her junior year at the University of Connecticut. She now teaches social studies at Daniel Hand High School.

Still another paragraph from a former student, Lynnea (Bidwell) Mahlke follows. This paragraph develops as an argument.

Businesses should focus on brochures as a main marketing tool. There are several advantages to using them. They contain detailed information, present the company in a professional manner, and can save us money on newspaper and magazine advertising. Due to their size, standard 8.5 × 11-inch, threefold brochures can convey more information than ads, direct-mail postcards, or flyers. Since they are usually printed on glossy paper, contain high-quality visuals, and present information in levels, they appear more professional than direct-mail postcards, flyers, or newsletters. Especially for an international company, postcards and flyers can give the impression that we are cutting costs or are not well established in the industry. Instead of spending money on large ads, we can use small ones that invite the prospective customers to call or write for a free brochure. This way the detailed information reaches people who are interested in our service, not everyone who reads a certain newspaper or magazine. These are the reasons that I have recently instructed the marketing department to design a brochure.

Arrangement of Details

A writer may arrange the details of a paragraph by time, order, comparison, contrast, comparison-contrast, space, or importance.

TIME

Since <u>1903</u>, Major League Baseball's championship has been decided by a World Series, sometimes best-of-nine-games, but mostly best-of-seven. There were two exceptions: The first occurred in <u>1904</u> when there were no games played, because either the manager, John McGraw, or the president of the New York Giants, John T. Brush, thought that the Red Sox of the American League were "inferior" and refused to play, and the second occurred in 1994—no Series because of the players' strike. <u>1907</u> witnessed the first tie game in World Series play; the second in 1912. In <u>1921</u>, the New York Yankees began their historic appearances in the World Series by losing five games to three to the New York Giants; <u>then</u> in <u>1922</u> the Giants swept the Yankees in four games. <u>The next year</u> the Yankees won their first Series and several more after that.

By Dan Mulvey

ORDER

Hitting a Major League fastball <u>begins</u> with the feet spread comfortably apart, toes parallel with the back edge of the plate, body relaxed. The batter <u>then</u> checks his grip on the bat, lining up the second joints of the fingers. <u>Next</u>, the elbows go up, and with each practice swing, the player concentrates on the ball of the back foot pivoting so that at the end of the swing the toe of the left foot is facing the pitcher. <u>At the same time</u> of the pivot, the hips turn to face in the direction of the pitcher. <u>Finally</u>, the follow-through ends with the bat in back with the back leg forming an "L."

By Dan Mulvey

COMPARISON

Hitler and Captain Ahab <u>share</u> a few characteristics. <u>Both</u> had charge of many different kinds of men, <u>both</u> inflicted their charisma on their underlings, and <u>both</u> leaders had one dominating thought that ultimately consumed them. Hitler and Ahab, known almost always by one name, were maniacal but not crazy, but they <u>both</u> wantonly caused nearly total human destruction with regard for no one. <u>They both</u> were physically handicapped but mentally powerful enough to sway the strongest of antagonists. In short, they might have been born from the <u>same</u> womb.

By Dan Mulvey

CONTRAST

Although Carl Sandburg and Robert Frost wrote poetry as contemporaries, their work <u>differs</u> greatly. First, Sandburg's poetry is nearly all free verse <u>while</u> Frost's poetry is rhymed and metered. Sandburg's most powerful scenes picture tough, city-hardened characters going about their business, <u>but</u> Frost's most touching scenes picture the quiet New England setting where farmers are mending walls or a young man is remembering the time he was swinging in birch trees. Also, <u>whereas</u> Frost concentrated mostly on poetry, Sandburg wrote for newspapers and compiled a multivolume biography of Abraham Lincoln.

By Dan Mulvey

COMPARISON-CONTRAST

Of the grand order of folio leviathans, <u>the Sperm Whale and the Right Whale</u> are by far the most noteworthy. They are the only two whales hunted by man. To the Nantucketer, they present the <u>two extremes</u> of all the known varieties of the whale. As the external <u>difference</u> between them is mainly observable in their heads. . . . In the first place, you are struck by the <u>general contrast</u> between these heads. <u>Both</u> are massive enough in all conscience, <u>but</u>, there is a certain mathematical symmetry in the Sperm Whale's which the Right Whale's sadly lacks. There is <u>more</u> character in the Sperm Whale's head. As you behold it, you involuntarily yield the <u>immense superiority</u> to him, in point of pervading dignity. In the present instance, too, <u>this dignity is height-</u>

<u>ened</u> by the pepper and salt color of his head at the summit, giving token to advanced age and large experience. In short, he is what the fishermen technically call a "grey-headed whale."

(from *Moby Dick,* by Herman Melville)

DESCRIPTION WITH DETAILS ARRANGED ACCORDING TO SPACE

Entering that gable-ended Spouter Inn, you found yourself in a wide, low, straggling entry with old-fashioned wainscots, reminding one of the bulwarks of some condemned old craft. <u>On one side</u> hung a very large oil painting so thoroughly besmoked, and every way defaced, that in the unequal cross-lights by which you viewed it, it was only by diligent study and a series of sympathetic visits to it, and careful inquiry of the neighbors, that you could any way arrive at an understanding of its purpose. Such unaccountable <u>masses of shades and shadows</u>, that at first you almost thought some ambitious young artist, in the time of the New England hags, had endeavored to delineate chaos bewitched. But by dint of much and earnest contemplation, and oft repeated ponderings, and especially by throwing open the little window <u>towards the back</u> of the entry, you at last come to the conclusion that such an idea, however wild, might not be altogether unwarranted.

(from *Moby Dick*, by Herman Melville)

ARGUMENT WITH DETAILS ARRANGED BY IMPORTANCE

A student should memorize and orally deliver pieces of literature for good reason. <u>First</u>, memorization of a poem or words of wisdom from a great author provides the student with the insight from a recognized source. <u>Second</u>, standing in front of a group of peers and interpreting someone else's words is good practice for the future, especially for experiences like job interviews. <u>Third, and most important</u>, the words memorized form the basis of the student's philosophy of living.

By Dan Mulvey

Transition

Transition is the bridge that connects ideas. Without attempting transition, the writer produces a disjointed, incoherent blather that makes no sense. Look back at the preceding paragraphs to understand how writers use transition to connect their ideas. Then read the paragraphs without those transitional expressions to see how important these connections are.

TRANSITIONAL EXPRESSIONS

Showing time

after a while, afterward, at last, at present, by the minute, currently, daily, during, eventually, on the hour, immediately, in the past, in the future, monthly, next, now, recently, soon, then, weekly, when, yearly

Showing order

first (second, third, etc.) but *not* firstly (or secondly, etc.), beginning, in the middle, last, then, next, after, before, finally

Showing comparison

again, also, and, as well as, both, in like manner, in the same way, likewise, similarly

Showing contrast

although, but, however, even though, in contrast, nevertheless, nor, on the contrary, on the other hand, or, otherwise, still, though, yet

Showing space

here, there, everywhere, beyond, to the left, to the right, in front of, on the side of, above, below, outside, inside, north (south, east, west), under, nearby

Showing importance

first, last, mostly, most important, more importantly

Task

Write several paragraphs where you arrange details in a specific pattern. Be sure each sentence has some kind of relationship with the sentence before it and the sentence after it. Use the preceding transitional expressions to keep the paragraph unified.

HOW TRANSITION OCCURS IN A PARAGRAPH

1. Transition occurs by using the transitional expressions to create smoothness and connection of ideas. The trick is to use these expressions wisely. Overuse causes clutter and redundancy. For example,

Dan and Doc were exact opposites. Dan, <u>on the other hand</u>, overflowed with enthusiasm. <u>Moreover</u>, he enjoyed life, he <u>also</u> loved people, and, <u>as well</u>, had fun. Doc, on the contrary, was more reserved, as well as serious, and <u>also</u> he was a solid newsman. . . . (Take the underlined transitional expressions out and there is a start of a good paragraph.)

(from the New Haven *Journal-Courier,*
July 20, 1963, an editorial about my father)

2. Use pronouns to connect sentences rather than repeat the same noun. If you are writing a paragraph, for example, about Althea Gibson, you would mention her name in the first (or the topic) sentence. After that mention, you then could use the pronouns "she," "her," or "hers" to refer to Althea.

3. Sometimes repeating the noun the paragraph is talking about emphasizes the point the author is trying to make. Also, by repeating the noun, the author clears up any reference of pronouns that might occur if there are several nouns in the sentences. Look at the beginning of a paragraph on basketball:

Basketball develops the mind as well as the body. Basketball demands simple equipment: one ball and a ten-foot high basket, with or without a net— even a chain-link net. Basketball, unlike golf, may involve several players at a time in the same game. Basketball . . .

4. Sometimes the general idea of the paragraph is enough to keep transition clear.

The digital camera makes conventional photography almost obsolete. Of course, great pictures depend on the number of pixels, those dots or triangles that compose the picture, and the more resolution one has with a digital camera the better the picture. The other day I bought a 3.1 million pixel camera, took about ten pictures, and every one came out beautifully. I did not have to send the film away, wait three weeks, and then get back several photos that were out of focus or otherwise nondescript. Rather, I downloaded the pictures onto the computer, touched up a few, and then printed $8\frac{1}{2} \times 11$ prints with a border. All except two were keepers, so I simply deleted them. No fuss, no mess.

By Dan Mulvey

Transition, then, is what holds the paragraph together. The better the transition, the clearer the ideas in the paragraph are presented. Transition is the visible (transitional expressions, etc.) or the invisible (the general idea of the paragraph) that makes writing, and reading understandable, organized, and pleasurable.

17

Developing One's Style

Style, *n.* . . . **2 a**: a distinctive manner of expression (as in writing or speech)
Merriam Webster's Collegiate Dictionary, 11th Edition

Developing a style culminates a writer's profession. Style separates one writer from another, and even separates periods of writing by the same author. For example, some of Herman Melville's first attempts at writing, in letters to his relatives, do not resemble, at all, *Moby Dick*; Emily Dickinson's first poem reads nothing like "Number 586" or like "Number 10"; Kurt Vonnegut's *Slaughterhouse Five* and *God Bless You, Mr. Rosewater* have only one common thread—no semicolons; but William Cullen Bryant reached his epiphany in his teens with his first published work on death, "Thanatopsis," a poem Richard Henry Dana thought was written by Dr. Bryant, William's father.

How does one develop style? Edna O'Brien in her fiction punctuates story lines with fascinating description:

Ahead of them the road runs in a long entwined undulation of mud, patched tar and fjords of green, the grassy surfaces rutted and trampled, but the young shoots surgent in the sun; flowers and flowering weed in full regalia, a carnival sight, foxglove highest and lordiest of all, the big furry bees nosing in the cool speckled recesses of mauve and white bell. O brazen egg-yolk albatross; elsewhere dappled and filtered through different muslins of leaf, an after-smell where that poor donkey collapsed, died and decayed; the frame of a car, turquoise once; rimed in rust, dock and nettle draping the torn seats, a shrine where a drunk and driven man put an end to himself, then at intervals rubbish dumps, the bottles, canisters and rank gizzards of the town riff-raff stowed in the dead of night.

This sample of writing, however, did not just all of a sudden appear. This writing results from a thorough understanding of grammar, vocabulary, and mechanics; in other words, this writer has put in time with words.

Emily Dickinson took language to another dimension. Without even mentioning a hummingbird, she captures its essence with

A Route of Evanescence,
With a revolving Wheel—
A Resonance of Emerald
A Rush of Cochineal—
And every Blossom on the Bush
Adjusts it's tumbled Head—
The Mail from Tunis— probably,
An easy Morning's Ride—

At first glance one sees mistakes: random capitalization (mostly nouns), dashes where other punctuation should go, cryptic phrases that take hours to grasp, the wrong use of "it's," and the puzzling allusion to "Tunis" in North Africa bordering the Mediterranean Sea. Also, the poem, Number 1489, does not mention the subject, the hummingbird. Further study of Dickinson reveals many poems like this one, poems that a reader may need help understanding. Her style differs radically from the roughness of John Greenleaf Whittier when in "Barbara Frietchie" he struggles with rhyme:

It shivered the window, pane and sash;
It rent the banner with seam and gash.
Quick as it fell, from the broken staff
Dame Barbara snatched the silken scarf.

And further on:

All day long that free flag tost
Over the heads of the rebels host.

No problem with "sash" and "gash," but he evokes cringes with "staff" and "scarf," to say nothing about "tost" (tossed) and "host." This poem is far more accessible than Dickinson's: A reader knows that an old lady has defended the flag against the enemy. Nearly all the couplets rhyme, and Whittier has told a story clearly about an historical event.

Herman Melville captured my interest long ago. Reading *Moby Dick* early on, I marveled at his vocabulary and the stories of the sea and the manner in which he interrupted the story line without frustrating the reader. In one of the many tense moments during a rescue of Tashtego, the Gay Head Indian who had fallen into a sinking spermwhale's head that had broken the tackle securing it to the side of the *Pequod*, Queequeg dives into the water to save old Tash. After the rescue, Melville playfully presents the reader with an astounding metaphor, one huge paragraph long. (Notice the tone of the passage and, of course, the last line.)

Now, how had this noble rescue been accomplished? Why, diving after the slowly descending head, Queequeg with his keen sword had made side lunges near its bottom, so as to scuttle a large hole there; then dropping the sword, had thrust his long arm far inwards and upwards, and so hauled out poor Tash by the head. He averred, that upon first thrusting in for him, a leg was presented; but well knowing that that was not as it ought to be, and might occasion great trouble;—he had thrust back the leg, and by a dextrous heave and toss, had wrought a somerset upon the Indian; so that with the next trial, he came forth in the good old way—head foremost. As for the great head itself, that was doing as well as could be expected.

Style, then, is as individual as a fingerprint, and developing style sometimes takes a lifetime to accomplish. By reading closely, you come to realize the differences in styles and to improve vocabulary at the same time. You should keep a journal and write every day; journals provide access to experimenting with language, fiddling with words and phrases and clauses, jotting here and jotting there, finding a way to say something just a bit differently. Read, read, read, and then read some more—and develop a broad vocabulary.

Developing a Vocabulary

Circling words in texts became a habit with me. Almost every book I own has some words circled and most also have a dictionary definition in the margin. Or, inside the front cover, there may be a list with words and page numbers so that I can find the words easily and look them up in context. Imagine sitting down to read "Bartleby the Scrivener" for the first time and encountering the following list:

Imprimis	Execrable
Prudence	Abate
Orbicular	Obstreperousness
Arduous	Verily
Abrogation	Restive
Advent	Insolent
Pursy	Temperate
Indecorous	Potations
Rash	Superfluous
Abridge	Paroxysms
Fervid	Alacrity
Sallow	Fain
Maledictions (twice)	Mollified
Ambiguous	Recondite
Ado	Pallidly

Forlorn (twice)
Sedate
Sanguine
Ignominiously
Gainsay
Paramount
Vouchsafed
Deferentially
Dyspeptic
Construe
Evinces
Mulish
Vagary
Pugilistic
Inveteracy
Wight
Dissipation
Tacit
Incipient
Deshabille
Incontinently
Effrontery
Decorous
Surmised
Chimeras
Pigeon holes
Refectory

Succor
Attenuated
Cadaverous (twice)
Aberration
Apprehension
Efficacy
Dispassionate
Bravado
Choleric
Hectoring
Rub (noun, like Hamlet's use of)
Inscrutable
Chafing
Altercation
Unhallowed
Construing
Obstreperous
Abated
Salutary
Billeted
Fathom
Obtrude
Incubus
Ere
Quiescent
Rockaway (twice)

Many of these words, students see on standardized tests and remember that they first saw the words when studying Melville. Also, students remember the recurring statement of Bartleby's, "I would prefer not to." But more important, reading stories like "Bartleby" and studying the vocabulary develops a "vocabulary awareness."

Ready to start?

1. Write some poetry. Try writing a sonnet, a poem of fourteen lines. Each line should contain ten syllables (iambic pentameter will not be mentioned here). The poem should be on a single subject.

2. Write some free verse. Free verse looks like poetry but is not structured with rhyme and meter. Poetic license allows freedom of expression, even coining words, like Emily Dickinson's "a convenient *grass*." Check out Walt Whitman's parallel structure techniques and his cataloguing of things observed.

3. If you're thinking of college, write a personal essay. Some colleges ask for short biographies or give a prompt to which you must respond. Go into the Guidance Office and peruse some college applications.

4. Be like Benjamin Franklin who learned to improve his writing by imitating Addison and Steele. Write an essay that imitates the rigorous style of a *Time* essay.

5. Find someone to read your writing. English teachers, math teachers, social studies teachers, science teachers, all can add certain contributions to your writing.

6. Write a short story that contains only action verbs, solid nouns, adjectives, and adverbs, and no indefinite pronouns.

7. Write a story where the use of the perfect tenses is necessary.

8. Hemingway was told that the only way a writer could improve would be to read only the works of dead authors. If William Cullen Bryant were alive today, he would say "Well, the person who told Hemingway has a point: There are more dead authors than live ones." (Read Bryant's "Thanatopsis," a poem written when he was about seventeen. In fact, his father, Dr. Bryant, found the poem in a desk drawer and sent it to Richard Henry Dana. Dana sent it back claiming that the father had written it, not the son.) Read, then, famous authors, dead or alive.

9. Write something every day. E-mail gives opportunities to experiment with those closest to you, those who might not be as critical as an English teacher. But write, write, write, write, and then some.

Standardized Tests

The bane of many students, standardized tests occur yearly and sometimes two or three times a year. There are two types of standardized tests: One measures the ability of a student compared with other students; the other measures a student's ability to apply knowledge learned. In general, these tests measure one's ability to write and in a larger sense to edit. Editing in this case does not mean to correct someone else's text, but it does mean to recognize sentence errors in diction (incorrect choice of words), expression (using idiom in place of correctness), grammar, and usage. Editing also means the ability to improve sentences and paragraphs that contain, besides the errors already mentioned, awkwardness of expression and errors in punctuation. This will be true whether the test is the ACT, the SAT, or any other standardized test on writing and sentence structure.

The following examples show the types of questions you may encounter. Try answering the questions before you check the answers.

EXAMPLE 1 **Combining Sentences**

Choose the best way to combine the two (or sometimes three) sentences:

Susan and Herbie Weber greet everyone warmly. No one leaves their house angry or hungry.

A. Susan and Herbie Weber greet everyone warmly, no one leaves their house angry or hungry.

B. Susan and Herbie Weber greet everyone warmly; no one leaves their house angry or hungry.

C. No one leaves their house angry or hungry: Susan and Herbie Weber greet everyone warmly.

D. No one at Susan and Herbie Weber's house leave angry or hungry.

ANSWER

The correct answer is B. The semicolon correctly connects and therefore combines the two sentences. Choice A is a classic run-on, C shows a misuse of the colon, and D has a subject-verb agreement problem.

EXAMPLE
2 **Choosing the best topic sentence for a paragraph**

The student is asked to select one of four answers that is the best topic sentence for a paragraph. In the following example, the first sentence has been omitted. Which of the four choices following this paragraph best serves as the topic sentence?

_____. This presentation allows the reader to glean what he or she needs to know in the first few sentences and decide whether to read on or move to the next story. Thus a first sentence might read: DOGPATCH, June 11—The fugitive wanted for the murder of eleven people was captured in an abandoned factory here, local police announced today. Increasingly, however, reporters write more like aspiring novelists than journalists, so the first sentence of the same story might read: DOGPATCH, June 11—The summer sun fades gently through the dusty haze of this Midwestern hamlet, where the prospect of murder is as distant as the shouts of Little Leaguers practicing on the field by the shuttered flywheel factory, an unsightly reminder of the town's faded industrial glory . . . .

A. The topic sentence of a paragraph should always be the first sentence.

B. Writing simply is writing best.

C. Straight facts are the best way to start a paragraph.

D. The proper structure of a news article, as any first-semester journalism student knows, is the inverted pyramid: the most salient facts on top, narrowing to important but nonessential information, and closing with finer details.

ANSWER

The correct answer is D. Choice A is false. Additionally, it is not a good choice because its tone is dictatorial rather than suggestive, as is the second sentence. Choice B may be true but it doesn't lead into the next sentence, which talks about presentation. Choice C may be true, but it's the presentation of facts, not the facts themselves, on which the paragraph concentrates. Choice D is the original topic sentence written by Stephen Allis, Harvard graduate and profuse writer. The sentence, a lesson in itself, prepares the reader for a salient technique in paragraph writing and is specific to a certain paragraph (the one presented), whereas the other choices are generalizations that may fit this paragraph and others waiting to be written but fall short for this example because they lack details and transition. This part of Allis's paragraph is presented with his permission.

EXAMPLE
3   **Choosing a sentence that does not belong in a certain paragraph**

Every sentence in a paragraph should have some connection to every other sentence in that paragraph. Which sentence in the following paragraph does not belong with the others?

(1) Reading Robert Frost is like hearing an old swamp Yankee spin yarns next to a potbellied stove. (2) His poetry, dominated by iambic pentameter and read slowly, resonates of a New England accent narration as in "Mending Wall": "Before I built a wall I'd ask . . . to whom I was like to give offense." (3) Robert Frost, "The New England Poet," was born in San Francisco. (4) The Down East touch of language materializes without fake devices. (5) Even the pun with the word "offense" hits the reader offhandedly, and tells the reader "Do not read too fast because you'll miss something."

ANSWER

Sentence 3 is the correct answer. Even though it is a true statement and interesting, this sentence interrupts the flow of the paragraph.

EXAMPLE
4   **Choosing a sentence that further develops the topic sentence**

From the answer choices given, select the sentence that best develops the following sentence.

Angling for blackfish (tautog, to many Easterners) takes total concentration and quick reactions.

A. These wily creatures, known also as practiced bait stealers, will take a hermit crab, green crab, or fiddler crab from a hook in the blink of an eye.

B. Bait is important in catching these good eating fish.

C. Drifting for these wily creatures is not the best way of fishing for them.

D. Anchoring in rock areas is the only way to catch them.

ANSWER

Choice A best adds to the first sentence because the words "practiced bait stealers" and "will take . . . from a hook in the blink of an eye" explain why "total concentration" is needed. Choice B is unrelated to the topic sentence, and it interrupts the flow of the paragraph to come. Choice C is irrelevant, and D, although important in this type of fishing, does not relate to the opening sentence, which talks about angling, not anchoring.

EXAMPLE
5
Identifying sentence errors

Choose the answer that contains an error. If there is no error, E would be your answer:

I knew <u>that</u> when the teacher had <u>spoke</u> to the class about the broken tape
      [A]   [B]
<u>recorder</u>, she was talking directly to Jack and <u>me</u>. <u>No error</u>
  [C]   [D]   [E]

ANSWER

The correct answer is B because a third principal part is demanded here. "Spoken" is the correct tense.

EXAMPLE
6
Improving sentences

This type of test measures your ability to recognize errors in sentence structure, punctuation, and usage; also tested is your ability to recognize effective writing. Either part of a sentence or the entire sentence is underlined. You are to determine if this underscore represents an error or correct standard English. Choice A repeats the original example, suggesting that the example is correct. The other four choices contain suggestions of correctness if there is, indeed, an error.

Example sentence:

The Alamo in San Antonio has always fascinated <u>historians that concentrate on Texas history.</u>

A. <u>historians that concentrate on Texas history.</u>

B. <u>historians, that concentrate on Texas history.</u>

C. <u>historians who concentrate on Texas history.</u>

D. <u>historians who concentrate on Texas History.</u>

E. <u>historians which concentrate on Texas history.</u>

ANSWER

The correct answer is C. The word "who" always refers to persons. Choice B is incorrect for two reasons: one is that the comma is not needed because what follows is a restrictive clause, and the other is that the word "that" does not refer to persons. Choice D is incorrect because "History" should not be capitalized. Choice E is incorrect because "which" always refers to inanimate objects and animals, not humans.

EXAMPLE
7

Improving a paragraph

To improve the paragraph below, choose the best correction of combining Sentences 4 and 5.

(1) The Littoral Society involves its members in programs that protect eco-systems, that survey fish population, that teach youngsters in marine science, and that restore marshlands and areas in danger. (2) Based in New Jersey, the Society's mission is "to promote the study and conservation of marine life and habitat, to defend the coast from harm, and to empower others to do the same." (3) One of their programs centers on tagging and releasing striped bass. (4) The angler who catches a tagged fish is asked to remove the tag and if possi-ble replace it with a new one. (5) Then send the original tag to the Society. (6) The Society in turn will send the angler a detailed report about the bass's vital statistics—where it was released, how long it is, and how big it is in pounds.

A. one. Then

B. one and then

C. one, then

D. one, however, then

E. one; and then

ANSWER

Choice B is the best combination because Sentence 5 is a fragment and should be attached to the previous sentence. You can't use Choice A because it remains a fragment. Choice C also remains a fragment, as does D. Choice E misuses the semicolon, separating a main clause from a subordinate clause.

EXAMPLE
8

Antonyms

Choose the word from the choices that is most nearly opposite in meaning to the word given:

CRAPULENT

A. forceful

B. meaningful

C. abstemious

D. restive

E. lascivious

ANSWER

If you said C, you are correct. "Crapulent" describes one with a drinking problem whereas "abstemious" describes one who is temperate in drinking (and eating, and so on). Choice A is incorrect because the opposite of "forceful" might be "lethargic." Choice B is incorrect because the opposite of "meaningful" might be "insignificant." The opposite of "restive," Choice D, might be "quiet." "Lacivious," Choice E, is a possible answer, but the word lacks the continuous feature of "crapulent."

EXAMPLE 9a   **Analogies (word relationships)**

See also the section on the colon in Chapter 19.
There are two types of analogies: one will ask you to supply one word, the end of a relationship; the other will ask for two words, a relationship itself.

Example: mail : armor :: saguaro :

A. flower

B. desert

C. cactus

D. giant

E. edible

ANSWER

The correct answer is C because "cactus" forms a proper relationship. Mail is a type of armor just as saguaro is a type of cactus. All the other choices apply to a saguaro cactus but they do not form the necessary relationship.

Try the next example:

EXAMPLE 9b

tommyrot : nonsense ::

A. unapt : fit

B. boneyard : cemetery

C. flatulent : modest

D. parsimony : generosity

E. vituperative : agreeable

ANSWER

The example, "tommyrot : nonsense" shows the relationship of two synonyms: "tommyrot" is slang for "nonsense." The only paired words in the answers that are similarly related are in Choice B. "Boneyard" is a slang word meaning "cemetery." Choices A, C, D, and E are antonyms.

THE ESSAY

All of these test examples have something to do with grammar, writing, or vocabulary. Grammar, writing, and vocabulary go together and should not be considered separate entities. If you wish to study exclusively for a particular test, log on to www.barronseduc.com *and you'll have more choices than a kid in a candy store. If you want to learn grammar to help your writing, go no further.* E-Z Grammar *is the book you need.*

There are tests that use some kind of prompt to generate a writing sample. These tests usually look like the following:

   Time allowed: 20 minutes

   Twenty minutes is not a long time to write an essay. The topic or prompt, usually from an identified source, must be agreed or disagreed with by the student. Here is an example of a prompt from The Great Gatsby, *by F. Scott Fitzgerald:*

Nick Carroway: "You can't repeat the past."
Gatsby: "Repeat the past? Why, of course you can."

I gave this quote to Nate Fischer's American Lit Honors section at Coginchaug Regional High School. Nate, a student of mine in 1998, gave his class the following hints:

1.   Take some time to outline your thoughts.

2.   As you begin writing, keep in mind that glaring errors aggravate the readers of these essays because most are English teachers, some retired. Therefore, please them with perfect grammar, spelling, diction, and punctuation.

3.   Make sure you understand the prompt. In this case you can agree with Nick or Gatsby.

4.   Do not begin sentences with "I believe" or "I think."

After twenty minutes, Nate collected the papers, handed them to me, and said, "Please evaluate these by tomorrow."

Tomorrow became three days later and the following essay by Emily Shoemaker stood out:

Although we may not have time machines or portals to alternate dimensions, we can still visit the past. Every child has keepsakes and memories that he grows up with, memories that allow him to relive his childhood and go back in time. Anyone can relive the past, if only in a small way.

As a child, I was taught that we all learn from our past mistakes. As we look back and try not to repeat transgressions and try to take good lessons to heart, sometimes the same bad things happen. Gatsby seems to think looking at the past is positive: "Can't repeat the past? Why, of course you can."

My grandmother said frequently, "Let's take a walk down memory lane." Whether recalling her first trip overseas or spending all day reminiscing over old photographs, my grandmother recalls, remembers, and visit's the golden days. Remembered places and photographs represent a way to be young again and stay with us as a key to the past.

Sure, old photos and life lessons may not be as useful as Hermione Granger's "Time Turner" from *Harry Potter and the Prisoner of Azkaban*, but they're treasured all the same—to remember the past.

I gave Emily a 5.8. There were virtually no errors, no usage mistakes, one misspelling, and possibly a missing conclusion; still, twenty minutes is not much time for a perfect paper. However, Emily came close.

Is there any other way to practice for these tests? You can time yourself at home, or you can ask that this practice be carried out in your classroom. Also, learn your grammar.

A Handbook of Mechanics–Punctuation and Capitalization

All You Need to Know About Punctuation

PERIOD

A *period* is the end mark signifying termination.

- Always put a period at the end of a sentence.

- Abbreviations sometimes need a period: St. Margaret, Conn. (but the postal code is CT with no periods); lat. 41 13′ 134″ long. 72 33′ 348″; 1st Lt., Lev. (Leviticus), sq. mi., Ph.D. However, sometimes abbreviations do not need a period: ESE, JFK, Pt (platinum—or any other element), YWCA, NAACP. Not sure about abbreviations? Three references are all one needs: *Webster's New Collegiate Dictionary*, Eleventh Edition; *The Chicago Manual of Style*, 15th Edition; and *American Heritage Dictionary*.

COMMA

A *comma* is a mark used to show a break in the action, a brief pause. There are a few steadfast rules a writer should follow, but commas are used mainly to clear up any construction that might not be understood without them.

- Use a comma with coordinating conjunctions (**and, but, or, nor, for,** and **yet**) to separate main clauses.

Jerry Davis emulates D. W. Griffith in movie production, **and** Kettie Davis, Jerry's wife, writes children's books.

Benny Davis keeps asking to become part of many scenes, **but** Ruby Davis will have none of it.

- Use commas to separate more than two main clauses.

D. J. Bennett plays baseball, Tyler Bennett runs track, Christopher Bennett participates in many sports, and Jake Bennett right now does not too much at all except "So Big."

- Use a comma to separate items in a series—including the item just before the conjunction.

With their employees Mike, Judy, Megan, Corrie, Sue, Carolyn, Kathy, Heidi, Marie, Alison, Michele, Michelle, and Liz, Dave and Holly Magee have owned and operated the Madison Coffee Shop for fifteen years.

Scott Paladino played football for the Hand Tigers, studied piano with several teachers, and distinguished himself permanently by delivering an address at graduation.

- Use a comma to separate an introductory adverb clause.

While he ran the car dealership in East River, Frank Paladino set many sales records.

After Doris Paladino took three lessons from Jim Piccolo, she broke par on her third attempt at eighteen holes.

- Use a comma to separate introductory adverb phrases (prepositional phrases) and introductory compound adverbs.

In the heat of the argument, Matthew Paladino shouted above the crowd.

By sitting near the exit of the theater, Gabriel Davis felt secure in case of fire.

Glumly but confidently, Stacey Paladino told the customer at the Unicorn that he should pay his bill and leave.

- Use a comma to set off introductory compound adjectives.

Tired and hungry, the mutt still wagged his tail in appreciation of the newly found shelter.

Parsimonious and rich, the miser chuckled at the poverty around him.

- Use a comma to set off introductory participial phrases.

Functioning as well as to be expected, John Schubert dug one hundred yews and drove them to Owego, New York.

Pouring drinks deftly, Dan continued to astound the patrons at Malone's.

- Use commas to set off expressions that interrupt the flow of the sentence or introduce a sentence.

Frank Paladino Jr., it has been told, once ate fourteen bowls of Wheatena when he was three.

Striped bass, without a doubt, caused the decline of baitfish in the harbor.

There was, after all, a time when life seemed a bit simpler.

I sat, however, through the entire boring performance.

No, I do not agree with that statement made by Stephen Michael Davis.

On the other hand, I recognize the inabilities of my most unworthy opponent.

- Use a comma to set off a nonrestrictive (nonessential) phrase or clause. Remember: A nonessential clause can be removed from the sentence, but that sentence will not change in meaning.

Keith Hotchkiss, who reads at least two novels a week, can quote hundreds of passages at a moment's notice.

The 2001 All-Star Game, which was played at Safeco Field in Seattle, featured a home run by Cal Ripken, Jr.

For restrictive clauses or phrases, no commas are needed:

The man <u>who donated three thousand dollars to the Jimmy Fund</u> remains anonymous.

The door prize was given to the woman <u>sitting in Aisle 6</u>.

The play <u>that determined the Mets' win in 1986</u> stands out in infamy for every Red Sox fan.

Note: Generally, use "which" to introduce a nonrestrictive clause and "that" for a restrictive clause. Also, if an essential clause is taken out of a sentence, the sentence meaning will change.

- Use a comma to set off direct address or an apostrophe (that is, talking to someone who is not present as if he were).

Gentlemen of the jury, have you reached a verdict?

I can't believe, Joe, that the tennis court you built is so beautiful.

God, please grant my wish.

Why have you done this, Bartholomew?

- Use a comma to set off a nonrestrictive appositive.

Hoyt Wilhelm, a pitcher for several Major League teams, hit a home run his first at-bat and then went over a thousand games without hitting another.

Terri James, the hostess with the mostest, serves up buffets that boggle the mind.

But notice the following:

My brother Mark drives a Mercedes.

Steinbeck's novel *Of Mice and Men* was first written as a play.

The adage "Spare the rod and spoil the child" seems not to apply to these times.

- Use commas in dates and addresses.

Larry and Betty O'Shea live at 124 Beechwood Drive, Madison, Connecticut.

On September 2, 1913, nothing took place at Meig's Point in Hammonasset.

Note: "2 September 1913" is acceptable without commas.

- Use commas to prevent verbal blunders.

To my mother, Gene was not to be trusted.

Just after, the bass that we released floated to the top and died.

Molly fought the bear that stormed into the room, and screamed.

SEMICOLON

The *semicolon* is stronger than a comma but not as powerful as a period. The semicolon indicates that what follows is related to what was previously stated, or it indicates that there are a few commas too many and the sentence needs clearing up.

- Use the semicolon to separate independent clauses.

Steve Bohan vacations in Nantucket for two weeks every year; he charters a boat and takes a few friends fishing there.

Mike Bohan claims that he can outfish anyone in the Tri-State area; so far, he has not caught a single fish, and his wife Patti constantly catches more than he does.

- Use the semicolon and transitional adverbs to make the relationship between two clauses absolute.

Students who do well on standardized tests usually do well in college; however, colleges look at more than standardized test scores.

Geoffrey MacLynn "Benny the Mop" Benbow specializes in restoring luxurious properties; moreover, his meticulous constructions have won him awards in *The Construction Journal*.

- Use the semicolon to clear up the use of many necessary commas.

The designated hitter rule, instituted by the American League, for whatever reasons, modernizes baseball, America's pastime; but purists agree that offensive strategy centered on the pitcher added intrigue to the game.

Dan dug ditches at Clinton Nurseries in Clinton, Connecticut; Art cut meat at Camp's Market in Madison, Connecticut; and Larry drove the highways as a State Trooper in Westbrook, Connecticut.

COLON

"Oh, two periods, one on top the other," defined one of my pupils, an exchange student from Brazil. This punctuation mark, in a sense, is nearly as strong as a period, but it does link one item with others (clauses, lists, relationships and hours, minutes, and seconds).

- Use a colon to introduce a list or a statement.

The principal decided to attempt a restructuring of discipline by this announcement to the students: First, you will arrive at school on time; second, you will report to homeroom immediately upon arrival; and third, you will consider the time between arrival and homeroom bell as study time.

My mother often quoted from Mark Twain: "The political and commercial morals of the United States are not merely food for laughter, they are an entire banquet."

(From an original script, a thesis paper, by Jack Lilburn—used with permission)
Bartender: Sorry, fella, you can't go in there.
Henry (frantic): I gotta call an ambulance!
Bartender: He don't need no ambulance, just some damn common sense. He's passed out here almost every night. Lives over in that shack. When he comes to, you tell him he's got a tab to pay for, not to mention a window.

Bring the following to the picnic: a grill, two tablecloths, a tape recorder, three baskets, and a blanket.

Rex Avery, once principal of Durham High School, posed three rules for every teacher to go by: First, she or he should be firm but fair; second, she or he should treat the students as humans, not as animals; and third, she or he should be in constant contact with the parents.

- Use a colon after a clause that is explained by the clause that follows.

Samantha Malone could not keep her luncheon date: She was flying to San Francisco later that day and had travel plans to consider.

Gene Monaco beamed as he entered the real estate office: He had just sold his house, which had been on the market for only two days.

- A colon is used in analogies on almost all major aptitude and achievement tests.

FOOLHARDY:CAUTION::

(A)   hardhearted:fear
(B)   careworn:anxiety
(C)   high-strung:tension
(D)   thick-skinned:sensitivity
(E)   spendthrift:resource

: = "is to" or "shows a relationship to"
:: = "as" or "just as" (the first word) shows a relationship to (the second word)

- A colon separates seconds from minutes and minutes from hours:

The record for the ten mile race at Camp Tahoova was 1 : 47 : 30 (one hour, forty-seven minutes, thirty seconds).

- In formal address, or in a letter to a person you are not familiar with, use a colon.

My fellow Americans:
Dear Sir:

- Do not use a colon when the list or the explanation is the complement or the object

No: We will serve for lunch: deep-fried oysters, whole belly clams, and a liverwurst sandwich with onions.

Yes: We will serve for lunch deep-fried oysters, whole belly clams, and a liverwurst sandwich with onions.

No: As we traveled through Connecticut we visited: Union, Southbury, Torrington, and Berlin.

Yᴇs: As we traveled through Connecticut we visited Union, Southbury, Torrington, and Berlin.

Nᴏ: On our next trip, we will travel to: Budapest, Prague, Vienna, and Salzburg.

Yᴇs: On our next trip, we will travel to Budapest, Prague, Vienna, and Salzburg.

DASH

Although used sparingly, the *dash* indicates an abrupt change in thought or an explanation or definition that seems to interrupt the flow of the sentence. The dash also is handy for emphasis when words are repeated.

As I trudged along—I could not get the thought out of my mind—concentration was out of the question.

When Whitney Malone—she was the one with the pony tail—spoke, everyone listened.

As the umpire called the infield fly rule—with runners at first and second or first, second, and third with fewer than two outs—the batter broke the bat in disgust because he was out.

We listened to Dr. Mel give the latest weather forecast of fair and mild—fair and mild, we have not seen that type of weather in several weeks.

QUOTATION MARKS

Quotation marks are used to indicate a direct speech; they are also set around the titles of poems (but not epics), chapters, short stories, and essays.

- Direct speech and interrupted direct speech.

"I won't go," said Joe.
Joe Fasone said, "I won't go."
"I won't go," said Joe, "because I'm slow."
"I won't go, said Joe. "I'm slow."
"I'm sick of this!" said Clo Davis. "Let's move on!"

- Indirect quotes need no quotation marks. "Indirect" means that the person or persons quoted said approximately, but not exactly, the words quoted:

Mike Katz and Jerry Mastrangelo state that Planet Fitness is all about total fitness in every aspect of the lives of the young and old. (What they might have said was "Planet Fitness is all about encouraging members to be totally fit in every aspect of their lives.")

Russell Allen Davis admonished that if I had waited one more second, I might have been better off. (What he might have said was "Wait a second!")

- Poems, and so on.

Ben Bruder recited "Two Tramps in Mudtime" (poem) but refused to recite it a second time.

Melville's chapter on whales, "Cetology," in *Moby Dick* gives the reader more information than he needs.

"The Secret Life of Walter Mitty" (short story) by James Thurber reminds me somewhat of my life.

Sir Francis Bacon's essay "On Studies" provides excellent advice on how to read a book.

- In a dialogue, each speech must be indented as if it were a paragraph.

". . . How much do a king git?"

"Get?" I says; "why, they get a thousand dollars a month if they want it; they can have just as much as they want; everything belongs to them."

"*Ain'* dat gay? En what dey got to do, Huck?"

"*They* don't do nothing! Why, how you talk. They just set around."

"No—is dat so?"

"Of course it is. They just set around. Except maybe when there's a war; then they go to the war. But other times they just lazy around; or go hawking."

From the *Adventures of Huckleberry Finn* by Mark Twain

THE APOSTROPHE

An *apostrophe* designates omission of a letter or letters, shows possession of some kind, and appears in plurals of most abbreviations and all numerals. Some critics argue that perhaps later on the apostrophe will be dropped, but the exclusion will cause more confusion than ever. Imagine "He'll be there" written as "Hell be there"!

Also, the apostrophe is a figure of speech that designates a person or thing spoken to whether the person or thing is present or not: "Death, be not proud," John Donne: "Rhodora, if the sages ask thee why," Ralph Waldo Emerson; "Tree at my window, window tree," Robert Frost.

OMISSION OF LETTER(S) AND SOUNDS—CONTRACTIONS

It's or 'tis—it is; bos'n, bo's'n, bo'sun—boatswain; couldn't—could not; we'll—we will; Hector's slain—Hector is slain; ha'—have; 'em—them; wasn't or was't—was not (Shakespeare contracted words to fit the meter as did most poets); ne'er—never; o'th' earth—of the earth; o'er—over; there's—there is; who's—who is; whose is possessive without the apostrophe.

POSSESSION

Linda Greenlaw's *Lobster Chronicles*; their hearts' desire; my heart's desire; children's room; geoduck's home; sheep's clothing (could be singular or plural depending on context); Pikes Peak is written without the apostrophe; conscience' sake; Moses' mother; Jesus' sake (but Jesus's sister); boy's world (singular); boys' dogs (plural); hers, ours, theirs but not her's, our's, their's.

Note: Some people avoid using the apostrophe with words ending in "s"; however, pronunciation tends to dictate "James's" or "Jesus's," for example.

PLURALS OF LETTERS AND NUMBERS AND AN OCCASIONAL WORD OR TWO

The 90s; in '75; two t's in little; three 15s in a row; Cs and Ds, but c's and d's, and M.A.'s and Ph.D.'s; the do's and don'ts of (don't's might be confusing).

Note: The illiterate or "grocer's apostrophe" (because one is more likely to see pear's and apple's at the grocer's store (rather than on a menu, for example) is usually on a handwritten sign by someone who should know better.

Task 31

Rewrite the following sentences if they contain an apostrophe or two that are either not needed or missing. If the sentence is correct, write "C."
(Answers on pages 186–187.)

1. Elizabeth Jo Mannings truck had two P's written on the windshield.

2. In the early 1980's, Sara Jo Manning was a figment of her parents imagination.

3. Samantha Grace Malones smile knocks out customer's at her fathers restaurant.

4. When the Mulv is bartending on Sunday, Lynne Marie Unitas need of a drink happens when the big guy checks out.

5. Its all right with Ashley Rose Unitas if Whitney Lincoln Malone take's her time getting to work.

6. Richard Stanford Messier's truck, after sixteen lobster bakes in a row, gets messier than a closet visited by a bull.

7. McHugh Martin Messier goes after the snapping turtle's eggs, and on Sundays, Malone's runs an omelette special.

8. Elizabeth Ann Messier's patience ran out when the deer in her front gardens constantly ate her impatiens.

9. Linda Greenlaws love of the ocean is evident in both her nonfiction and her fiction.

10. When Jeffrey John Manning left for a business trip, his wife packed his bag's with Mar's bars and chocolate chips.

All You Need to Know About Capitalization

NAMES OF PERSONS AND THINGS

- Capitalize the name of a person or the name of a particular object.

Linda Neale
John F. Kennedy Airport (or JFK Airport)
Chris W. Simmons
Mark Van Doren; Van Doren
Fortier von Sumac; von Sumac
George Washington Bridge (or GW Bridge)
Bryant Park
Massachusetts Institute of Technology (or MIT)
Metropolitan Transit Authority (MTA)

- Capitalize titles and offices.

President Lincoln
President (always capitalized when referring to the President of the United States)
Lawyers Snow and Costello
Senator Dodd, a senator from Connecticut

- A particular location is capitalized.

East (North, South, West) when referring to sections of the country
east (west, north south) when referring to directions
Panhandle
East Side (in New York)
East River (a section in Madison, Connecticut)
Moosehead Lake
Right Bank (in Paris)
Walden Pond
Lake Ontario
The French Alps
Leaning Tower of Pisa

- The names of companies and organizations are capitalized.

Japan Tobacco
Gateway
Hudson River Foundation
Girl Scouts of America
Holy Alliance
World Gym

For the most complete list of capitalization categories, see *The Chicago Manual of Style.*

Task 32

The following sentences are either correct or contain one to three errors in punctuation or capitalization. Place a "C" next to the correct sentences. If the sentence contains one or more errors, rewrite it correctly. (Answers are on page 187.)

1. Grover Whalen, Manhattan's perennial greeter and president of New York's Worlds Fair summered in Madison, Connecticut next to the East Wharf beach.

2. During the Vernal Equinox, winter flounder flatfish to the novice, begin feeding voraciously along the Beaches of Long Island Sound.

3. James Thurber, on June 16, 1928, published a Short Story, "Advice to American Ladies," in that weeks "New Yorker."

4. Joe Bruno once ate fifteen hamburgers with onions and ketchup; moreover, Joe does many other things, but it's okay because he does them himself.

5. Gene Rip Calzetta a local barber of renown once fell asleep on the top of a subway car in Grand Central station.

6. Please give the tautog to: Louie Santanelli and his brother Richie before they sic the mob on you, pleaded Tim Malone.

7. Michael Lucas, who owns Guilford's Star Fish Market with his wife, Colette, says there are five deliveries of seafood each week to ensure off-the-boat freshness.

8. Editing the copy of the new Magazine River & Shore Dennis Bell found several grammatical errors in the article about Cedar Island.

9. A. Melissa Frey shouted, "Why are Teresa Jones and Robin White fighting!"
   B. Robin looked up from the floor and replied—heatedly—"Can't you see"!
   Which one is correct?

10. If the Chief was disabled, why would the town grant him nearly one hundred grand? was the question on most thoughtful taxpayers minds.

A Word or Two About Spelling

"Remember! Spelling counts!" Of course as one passes on through the school system, teachers sometimes disregard the topic of spelling completely but hack away at the grades of the poor speller. At the college level, some papers are graded "F," like the essay on *The Iliad* that had the work in question spelled "Illiad." Even before college, the admissions officer chooses the perfectly spelled essay but tosses the bad ones to the trash. Then, later on, in applying for the job that requires a modicum of writing, the poor speller is told to hit the road.

On the other hand, there live those teachers who believe that poor spelling does not a bad student make. One English teacher in Europe handed back an "A" paper (three pages) that had twenty-five glaring spelling errors. When questioned by the parent, an English major in college, about the discrepancy, the teacher responded, "I did not want to hurt his self-esteem." Or the other teacher who said, "I couldn't spell as a child so why should I penalize my students who can't spell?"

As Kurt Vonnegut might say, "So it goes."

The nonthreatening approach to better spelling might include the following plan for the teacher and the student.

1. While correcting any writing the student does, circle spelling errors.

2. The student is to find the correct spelling of the word by looking in the dictionary, by asking someone, or by having the teacher write the correct spelling on the returned paper.

3. The student then writes the correct spelling five times in a notebook.

Another solution came from Art Donaldson, a former teacher in the Madison Public Schools (in Connecticut): He theorized that a poor speller could get better if he typed all his homework—there were no computers with "spell check" then—because the student would have to find the letters one at a time and therefore at least initially (no pun intended) begin the long road to correct spelling.

Here is a list of words students often misspell:

Wrong	Correct
accidently	accidentally
accomodate	accommodate
amoung	among
bellweather	bellwether
calender	calendar
concientious	conscientious
definately	definitely
durring	during
existance	existence
grammer	grammar
harrass	harass
indispensible	indispensable
innoculate	inoculate
miniscule	minuscule
mischievious	mischievous
mispell	misspell
ocurred	occurred
paraphanalia	paraphernalia
pasttime	pastime
priviledge	privilege
questionaire	questionnaire
seperate	separate
supercede	supersede
supposably	supposedly
ukalele	ukulele
withold	withhold

"The Final" or "The Beginning"

The purpose of this chapter is twofold: One, the following items represent what you might have learned during a systematic approach to *E-Z Grammar*; two, these items may serve as a diagnostic test so that you may use the results to brush up on those items that in the past confused. In addition, these sentences need not be done in order. In fact, perhaps the best way to approach this test is with lack of order. The answers in Appendix 1 will give a brief explanation of the error.

100-Item Grammar Final

The following sentences contain errors of those sentence elements discussed in this text. Identify the error or errors according to the following letters; then correct the sentence by changing the incorrect part(s) or by rewriting the sentence. (Answers are on pages 187–193.)

A—Correct sentence
B—Misplaced or dangling modifier
C—Incorrect coordination or subordination
D—Lack of parallel structure
E—Lack of agreement: subject-verb
F—Lack of agreement: pronoun-antecedent
G—Reference of pronoun error
H—Incorrect case of pronoun
I—Incorrect tense, mood, or verb form
J—Passive voice needs to be changed to active voice
K—Fragment
L—Run-on

M—Usage mistake

N—Punctuation error (other than a comma)

O—Comma error

P—Spelling error

Q—Redundancy

R—Capital letter mistake (one is needed or not needed)

S—Unnecessary shift in person

T—Incorrect use of comparative or superlative

1. In the month of May just when the weather breaks and the water temperature in Long Island Sound reaches 50 degrees.

2. Michelle and Judy Daricek, although twins from birth, do not think alike.

3. Yankee Stadium the "House That Ruth Built" acommodates huge crowds lately because George Steinbrenner has bought the best in baseball.

4. Kim Davis, along with several of her closest friends, often visit the Baseball Hall of Fame in Cooperstown New York.

5. Bill Breck the Superintendent of Schools in Durham Connecticut announced that Tom Purcell, one of the stellar teachers in the system would receive full retirement and health coverage based on his tenure in the system.

6. When boarding the "f" train that goes to Brooklyn, it's better to wait for one that isn't crowded.

7. Dressed in nothing but a nightgown, the burglar froze when he saw the woman with a shotgun.

8. When Bob Betterini walked in the meeting room, a hush fell upon the people already there.

9. Wally and Judy Camp vacation for six months in Naples, Florida, they both play golf every day.

10. During the writing of his autobiography about his life in Elmira, New York, Mark Twain told some stories about the amount of people that used to visit him.

11. As he listened intently to the speaker rambling on about his adventures in Berlin, Charlie Rogers took notes furiously so he wouldn't miss anything.

12. Candy Brickley taught home economics 101 for thirty years after she earned her Master's Degree from Mississippi State.

13. Albie Booth, Yale's diminutive captain and star, grasped opportunity by the forelock today, hung on with the tenacity of a bulldog, which is the mascot of his college, and carried through to beat Harvard by a score of 3-0.

14. To frolic in the puckerbrush and enjoying nature to its fullest, is what makes me look forward to retirement.

15. If Harold Eddy was to invest in Oracle, Abbott Labs, and Pfizer, he would make a fortune.

16. Whenever Richard Cory went downtown, we people on the pavement looked at him.

17. Maureen Scheppach and I took a vacation to the south of France where some local merchants gave wine cases to her and I.

18. Although Danny Fitzgerald sometimes does not eat his supper the way he is supposed to, especially on Saturday afternoon when the cartoons are on.

19. "If the wind's from the east, the fishing's the least" says an old adage but it goes on to say that if the wind's from the west, the fishing's the best.

20. Brilliant, beautiful, charming, ebullient, Jackie Catania is my friend for almost forty years.

21. We have caught less fish this year then we did last year.

22. Jim Martin announced this year he was going to purchase the biggest motoryacht that Bayliner made.

23. In her illustrious career as a teacher, Nancy Martin not only captured the hearts of her students but also she reigned as the queen of the teacher's room.

24. If someone would concentrate a little more at the workstation, they would find that the operation of the plant would be smooth.

25. Ken Griffey Jr., as well as some of the other players traded by the Seattle Mariners, wish they were back where they came from.

26. Most viewers agree that "The Crocodile Man" is very unique in its format.

27. Taking pictures with a digital camera alleviates the taking of the film to the store to be developed, but to find one that works correctly daunts most buyers.

28. A work that aspires, however, humbly, to the condition of art should carry its justification in every line.

29. Horton Smith, although not exactly a household name in the world of golf, won the first Masters Tournament with a score of 284 which stood as a record for one year.

30. Gouache, a method of watercolor painting, artists use when they want to produce a less transparent effect.

31. The machine gun, discovered in 1862 by Richard Jordan Gatling, furnished several armies with an extremely destructive weapon.

32. The Language-Arts Committee met in the hall next to the auditorium that discussed plans for the five-year mission to rebuild the program.

33. Lake Leman woos me with its crystal face, the mirror where the stars and mountains view the stillness of their aspect in each trace its clear depth yields of their far height and hue.

34. If one were to look from the empire state building into central park, she would see what looks like a jungle.

35. Bessie Smith, who was born in Tennessee, sometimes by experts is considered the greatest Blues Singer of all time.

36. Visitors to the Blue Note in the Village the place where many tourists go to hear the best jazz in the world sometimes are disappointed in the brunch served on Sundays.

37. "What time is it," asked the conductor. "Twelve-thirty." said the passenger.

38. Skiers in France should take extra care, especially when you are in Chamonix.

39. While driving in France, the operator of the vehicle must be aware that the left side of the highway is for passing only; subsequently, other drivers will blink their lights if a car refuses to move into the right-hand lane.

40. In Ireland, driving on the left side of extremely narrow roads outside of Cork or Dublin, and even on some of the new highways where there is not much to see.

41. The narc spotted the drug paraphanalia in the back seat of the suspect's minivan.

42. These kind of reels made by Shimano are better than the same type made by Penn.

43. My sister received a shipment of pearls from Ukraine in a box labeled "FRAGILE."

44. If someone wanted to introduce you to Karol Wojtyla, you probably would not think much of the meeting the name that you would know and might get you excited would be Pope John Paul II.

45. One of the Seven Wonders of the Ancient World is the Mausoleum at Halicarnassus in Turkey, which never ceases to amaze visitors.

46. In 1947 The Philadelphia Warriors defeated the Chicago Stags in the first National Basketball Championship Series.

47. For my new neighbor and I, the rest of the neighborhood threw a party that lasted fourteen days.

48. Since I was stuck with several bottles of wine, I gave them to whomever had enough room to carry them.

49. At Fenway Park, fans cheer like there is no tomorrow because they now have something to cheer about.

50. Taking no chances, the children at Jeffrey Elementary School were innoculated five times in one year.

51. Words to the heat of deeds too cold breath gives.

52. In January, 1967, during Super Bowl I between the Green Bay Packers and the Kansas City Chiefs and millions of fans watching on television.

53. One time my daughter Erin and I during a return flight from Los Angeles saw Jack Kramer the 1947 Men's Singles Champion at Wimbledon walk by us.

54. The Congress shall have power to lay and collect taxes, duties, imposts and excises, to pay the debts and provide for the common defense and general welfare of the United States; but all duties, imposts and excises shall be uniform throughout the United States.

55. In 1955, Rosa Parks not only refused to move to the back of the bus but also she, without knowing it, brought national awareness to one of America's festering sores.

56. What does August, sardonyx, and poppy have in common? Sardonyx is the birthstone and poppy the flower for the month of August.

57. Venus and Earth are nearly equidistant from the sun and no one lives on Venus that we know of.

58. Aram Khachaturian although not well known is famous for *Gavane* a ballet and from that work of course *Sabre Dance* a song which is recognizable.

59. Teodor Jozef Konrad Korzeniowski was the real name of Joseph Conrad, author of *Lord Jim* and *The Secret Sharer.*

60. Dean Bennett Jr. plays golf better than any person in the Madison Country Club, according to Mickey Hawkes, the resident pro.

61. Gerald Birnbaum, Madison's gardening-expert-answer to Martha Stewart and many others, plant tomatoes early in April and pray for no frost.

62. Even though he had casted several times, Art Schneider retrieved nothing from the Mystic River accept an old boot.

63. Rob Gourley has been a sailor for the last thirty years and now has switched to motorboating.

64. Because the aspiring student thought he had mispelled a word on the questionaire, he figured his chances of enrolment were slim.

65. When our vacation was cut short because of a one-day strike by Aer Lingus in Ireland, our travel agent made quick arrangements for us to fly back to New York.

66. The aspirin tablets are in the medicine cabinet if you need one.

67. That kind of a reel makes it more difficult for me to land the fish.

68. For her and I to leave Paris at noon and then fly to Geneva for a connecting flight to Rome, the exhaustion is just too much to think about.

69. Fred Parker took tour groups to Turkey, worked in Manhattan during most weeks, and was a member of the Madison Beach Club.

70. When stopping in Crooksville, Ireland, for a pint at Clifford's, tourists ought to visit the grave of Michael Collins, which is about a mile and a half from the pub.

71. If you ever go across the sea to Ireland and drive around the ring of Kerry, stop in Smeen and have a pint or two at The Blue Bull give Kathleen O'Connell greetings from the United States.

72. On our way to Ballybunion, where a statue depicts Bill Clinton about to tee off near Shannon airport after a brief stop at Avis to upgrade the car that was too small for our luggage.

73. Of the two former super stars, Oscar Robertson and Elgin Baylor, Robertson reigned the best in shooting but Baylor dominated in several categories including assists and rebounds.

74. When the secretary of state met with the speaker of the house Tip O'Neill, he discussed foreign policy until they were interrupted by the arrival of the president.

75. One of my three hundred pound friends stun audiences with the amount of hot dogs he can consume at one sitting.

76. To write The Great American Novel, to climb higher than any other adventurer, and formulating ideas that will benefit mankind is the goal of many college graduates.

77. If Richie the mechanic brung his tool box when he left for the boat show in Newport, perhaps the breakdown of the travel lift could have happened earlier than it did.

78. The tremulous sea itself, when I could find sufficient pause to look at it, in the agitation of the blinding wind, the flying stones and sand, and the awful noise, confounded me.

79. Frank Howard who played Major League Baseball while at Ohio State set a rebounding record for the Holiday Festival in New York.

80. Alyssa Davis sells marine insurance to qualified boaters although she believes protection of the craft is a necessity.

81. The culprit who pulled the fire alarm must have trouble with their self-esteem.

82. The man listed his name and address as Dominic Serafino 382 Percival Avenue Kensington Connecticut.

83. Through Alpine meadows soft-suffused with rain, where thick the crocus blows, past the dark forges long disused, the mule track from Saint Laurent goes.

84. Arthur Godfrey played the ukelele seperately from the band because he said they could not stay with him.

85. Some people keep the Sabbath going to church, I keep it staying at home with a boblink for a chorister and an orchard for a dome.

86. Many whalers thought certain species ubiquitous since they were seen, supposedly, in different parts of the world at the same time.

87. The School Building Committee thought that a new high school would solve the town's education problems the real solution, however, turned out to be the hiring of qualified staff.

88. Frantic searches for the missing girl both by the National Guard and by the local volunteer fire department failed to turn up any clues to her whereabouts.

89. In the local high school, industrial arts programs were done away with because of lack of budget, which caused many residents alarm.

90. In the Nineteen Hundreds, basic rules of society seemed to change, but then in the Two Thousands experts began to see a change for the better.

91. In the open room upon the courtyard of the Palazzo Vitelleschi lie a few sarcophagi of stone, with the effigies carved on top, something as the dead crusaders in English churches.

92. If the data is removed from the file, the police will have no leads.

93. If the teacher had accepted my three lowest grades, I would have passed the course.

94. Read not to contradict and confute, nor to believe and take for granted, nor to find talk and discourse, but to weigh and consider.

95. One of my favorite flowers, the black-eyed susan, smells much nicer than does the new England aster.

96. Each participant in "The Weakest Link" should have nerves of steel and a thick skin to make it through their ordeal.

97. I should have went to the movies instead of staying home because my wife made me cut the lawn.

98. After the game, several of my friends and I retired to the Lexington Avenue Pub: four hours later we decided to take the off-peak train home to New Haven.

99. Close by those meads, forever crowned with flowers, where Thames with pride surveys his rising towers, there stands a structure of majestic frame, which from the neighboring Hampton takes its name.

100. When I taught English, some of the best errors to present on tests came from those dicta from the Board of Education, all sorts of errors blotched the papers from that office: agreement problems, lack of parallel structure, spelling errors, etc.

A1

Appendix 1: Answers

Task 1

Pages 3–4, Chapter 1, The Sentence, Finding the subject and verb

1. (Roxie Murphy Strachbein), from Orthodontics on the Plateau, (used to live in Durham, Connecticut.)

2. Ripping a phone book in half, (Victor Engel)(wanted to impress his dramatics class.)

3. (Gerry Degenhardt), rummaging in the attic, (found a photo album filled with pictures of Chuck Collins.)

4. (Charles Edward Lipnicki), along with Robert Judson "The Stalker" Turton), (plays with people's minds incessantly.)

5. (Dennis Mullin), once a liberal, (has turned into one of the biggest conservatives.)

Task 2

Page 7, Chapter 1, The Sentence, Correcting fragments and run-ons

1. F   Because F. Scott Fitzgerald had to return the publisher's advance for *The Great Gatsby*, he fell into a deep depression.

2. R   Machen Dolan worked out at World Gym with his favorite teacher. She pulled a muscle, however, and later sued his family. (2 sentences)

   Machen Dolan worked out at World Gym with his favorite teacher; she pulled a muscle and later sued his family. (Two main clauses separated by a semicolon)

Machen Dolan worked out at World Gym with his favorite teacher, but she pulled a muscle and later sued his family. (Two main clauses separated by a comma and a conjunction)

Machen Dolan worked out at World Gym with his favorite teacher; however, she pulled a muscle and later sued his family. (Two main clauses separated by a semicolon, a comma, and strong connector)

Machen Dolan worked out at World Gym with his favorite teacher who pulled a muscle and later sued his family. (One of the clauses is subordinated with the relative pronoun "who.")

3. C   Both main clauses are short enough and related enough so that the writer does not need a comma before the conjunction "and."

4. F   Since Bob Sullivan has served on the Board of Directors for the Madison Country Club, the club's assets have tripled.

5. C

6. F   During the month of May and several days into the month of June, rain battered the East Coast.

7. C

8. F   Bob "Andrew" Zingone, frequently goading bartenders into telling the most outrageous jokes about feminism and the Reconstruction of the South, aggravates the patrons around him.

9. F   Sandra Beach Barry, strolling down Madison Avenue near 48th Street in Manhattan, near the exclusive store where she used to shop, found a wallet stuffed with thirty thousand dollars.

10. R   Joe Peter Votto built a house in Buffalo Bay. Before he built that house, he had lived in Queens. (two separate sentences)

Joe Peter Votto built a house in Buffalo Bay, but before he built that house, he had lived in Queens. (two independent clauses joined by a comma and conjunction)

Joe Peter Votto built a house in Buffalo Bay; before he built that house, he had lived in Queens. (two main clauses separated by a semicolon)

Joe Peter Votto built a house in Buffalo Bay; however, before he built that house, he had lived in Queens. (two main clauses separated by a semicolon and a strong connector)

Before he built a house in Buffalo Bay, Joe Peter Votto had lived in Queens. (one of the clauses subordinated to the other)

Task 3

Pages 14–15, Chapter 2, Parts of Speech, Finding the subject (Verbs are in parentheses.)

1. parents (listen)

2. Costy (slammed, left)

3. Dan Zeoli (pulled)

4. Classic and Spider Solitaire (divert)

5. World Gym (offers)—main clause; payment (accompanies)—dependent clause.
   Note: "discount" is the direct object of "offers."

6. spending (exceeds)

7. Lobstermen (were compensated)

8. *Fowler's Modern English Usage* and *The Chicago Manual of Style* (provide)

9. thought (lurks)

10. Herb and Gaye Weber (felt)

Task 4

Page 16 for directions, pages 14–15 for the sentences, Chapter 2, Parts of Speech, Finding the direct object

1. No direct object

2. games (direct object of "losing," a gerund); cards

3. muscle

4. attention

5. discount

6. monies

7. No direct object

8. information

9. No direct object

10. something

Task 5

Page 17 for directions, pages 14–15 for the sentences, Chapter 2, Parts of Speech, Finding the indirect objects

5. *body builders*—If the writer were to put "to" or "for" in front of "body builders," then "body builders" would be the object of the preposition.

8. *writers*—The "for" is missing.

There are no more indirect objects in these two sentences.

Task 6

Page 22, Chapter 2, Parts of Speech, Finding adjectives and adverbs

1. adverbs—*Carefully* (modifying "put"); adjectives—*one* (modifying "foot"); *the* and *thin* (modifying "ice"); *its* (modifying "safety")

2. adverbs—*accidentally* (modifying "smashed"); adjectives—*running* (modifying "Sam" and "Matthew"); *the* (modifying "house"); *some* and *valuable* (modifying "crystal")

3. adverbs—*definitely* (modifying "think"); adjectives—*Many* (modifying "fishermen"); *beautiful* (modifying "LIS"); *only* (modifying "theirs")

4. adverbs—*instantly* (modifying "recognized"); *safely* (modifying "steered"); adjectives—*Marvelous* (modifying "Marvin Murphy"); *the* and *hidden* (modifying "shoal"); *the* (modifying "east")

5. adverbs—*strangely* (modifying "behaved"); adjectives—*the* and *neighborhood* (modifying "dogs"); *a* and *five pound* (modifying "bag")

6. adverbs—*stubbornly* (modifying "doubted"); adjectives—*the* (modifying "bartender"); *a* and *grammar* (modifying "book")

7. adverbs—*best* (modifying "tasting"); *ever* (modifying "eaten"); adjectives—*Black* (modifying "seabass"); *the* and *tasting* (modifying "fish")

8. adverbs—*extensively* (modifying "toured"); adjectives—*Mixing* (modifying "Bob Sullivan"); *neighboring* (modifying "towns")

9. no adverbs; adjectives—*the* (modifying "NYM")

10. adverbs—*moderately* (modifying "chastised"); adjectives—*Decorous* and *quiet* (modifying "Kippy Martin"); *her* and *daughter's* (modifying "teacher")

Task 7

Page 24, Chapter 2, Parts of Speech, Identifying the parts of speech

1. <u>moment</u>—noun (subject)
2. <u>not</u>—adverb
3. <u>by</u>—preposition
4. <u>Only</u>—adverb
5. <u>lone</u>—adjective
6. <u>that</u>—demonstrative adjective
7. <u>He</u>—pronoun
8. <u>who</u>—relative pronoun
9. <u>waited</u>—verb
10. <u>lurked</u>—verb
11. <u>made</u>—verb
12. <u>preparations</u>—noun (direct object)
13. <u>should be</u>—verb
14. <u>through</u>—preposition
15. <u>strong</u>—adjective
16. <u>two-inch</u>—adjective
17. <u>and</u>—conjunction
18. <u>door</u>—adjective
19. <u>softly</u>—adverb
20. <u>box</u>—adjective
21. <u>had gimleted</u>—verb
22. <u>upholstered</u>—adjective
23. <u>toward</u>—preposition
24. <u>one-shot</u>—adjective
25. <u>eight-ounce</u>—adjective
26. <u>winged</u>—adjective (past participle)
27. <u>He</u>—pronoun (subject)

28. <u>every</u>—adjective

29. <u>lengthened</u>—verb

30. <u>away</u>—adverb

Task 8

Page 24, Chapter 2, Parts of Speech, Using all the parts of speech in as few words as possible

"Bosh!" she exclaimed. "In the middle of an exciting adventure and mystery a commercial appears."

Noun—<u>middle</u>

Pronoun—<u>she</u>

Adjective—<u>exciting</u>

Verb—<u>exclaimed</u>

Adverb—<u>In the middle</u> (prepositional phrase modifying "appears")

Preposition—<u>of</u>

Conjunction—<u>and</u>

Interjection—<u>Bosh</u>

Task 9

Pages 27–28, Chapter 3, Phrases, Selecting prepositional phrases

1. *On his way* (adverb, modifying "witnessed"); *to the gym* (adjective, modifying "way"); *with a motorcycle* (adverb, modifying "collide")

2. *Behind the elm tree* (adverb, modifying "discovered"; *near the movie theater* (adjective, modifying "tree); *in the shape* (adjective, modifying "purse"); *of an ear* (adjective, modifying "shape")

3. *In spite of his efforts* (adverb, modifying "continued"); *on the scratch-off tickets* (adverb, modifying "to lose") Note: "to win" and "to lose" are infinitives, not prepositional phrases.

4. *Throughout her college career* (adverb, modifying "dazzled") *with her outstanding achievements* (adverb, modifying "dazzled")

5. *Until recently* (adverb, modifying "worked"); *as an analyst* (adverb, modifying "worked"); *in London, England* (adverb, modifying "worked")

6. *Without a moment's hesitation* (adverb, modifying "pulled" and "married"); *at a university* (adverb, modifying "teaches"); *in Israel* (adjective, modifying "university")

7. *beyond their limits* (adverb, modifying "go") Note: "to help" is an infinitive.

8. *During the exhibition* (adverb, modifying "scattered"); *at the local high school* (adjective, modifying "exhibition"); *over the parking lot* (adverb, modifying "scattered")

9. No prepositional phrases

10. *Upon hearing* (adverb, modifying "suggested"); *of woe* (adjective, modifying "tale"); *to him* (adverb, modifying "confessing"); *from the youth officer* (adjective, modifying "help")

Task 10

Page 32, Chapter 3, Phrases, Identifying phrases

1. *Navigating through Plum Gut* (participial phrase, modifying "Bobby Bushnell"); *through Plum Gut* (prepositional phrase, modifying "Navigating"); *around the Tea Pot* (prepositional phrase, modifying "Bobby Bushnell"); *for Lake Montauk* (prepositional phrase, modifying "heading")

2. *by selling* (prepositional phrase, modifying "set"); *selling fourteen motoryachts in a six month period* (gerund phrase, object of the preposition "by"); *in a six-month period* (prepositional phrase, modifying "selling"); *the man . . . Bayliners* and other brands (appositive phrase)

3. *To help me in my new sales career* (infinitive phrase, modifying "Marshall Corona"); *in my new sales career* (prepositional phrase, modifying "To help"); *of selling* (prepositional phrase, modifying "secrets").

   Note: "selling" is a single-word gerund, the object of the preposition "of."

4. *After a grueling day* (prepositional phrase, modifying "was treated"); *at the Norwalk Boat Show* (prepositional phrase, modifying "day"); *to a grand supper* (prepositional phrase, modifying "was treated"); *at MacDonald's* (prepositional phrase, modifying "was treated")

5. *Not watching what he was doing* (participial phrase, modifying "Dwight Palmer"); *of the staircase* (prepositional phrase, modifying "steps")

   Note: "what he was doing" is a noun clause, the object of "watching."

Task 11

Pages 32–33, Chapter 3, Phrases, Identifying phrases and their uses

1. G   object of "tried" and therefore a noun phrase
2. A   adverb modifying "were shackled"
3. C   modifies "policemen"
4. A   adverb modifying "stood"
5. B   modifying "murmur"
6. C   modifying "eyes"
7. C   modifying "face"
8. A   modifying "oval"
9. C   modifying "Mrs. Dalton"
10. A   modifying "moment"
11. C   modifying "Bigger"
12. C   modifying "fingers"
13. G   modifying "pressing"

Task 12

Page 33, Chapter 3, Phrases, Writing sentences according to the phrase directions
Suggested answers appear here:

1. In the middle of the night, Mary Walby awoke from a deep slumber to let the cat out of the house.

2. Rummaging through the attic for a lost baseball card, Greg Walby found a purse full of gold lying on a cardboard box.

3. Subject: Singing in the shower bolsters my ego.

   Direct object: Chris Walby began casting off Middle Beach near Tom's Creek and landed a forty-five-inch striped bass.

   Indirect object: Chuck Walby gave riding horseback not much of a fling.

   Object of the preposition: By laughing at the wrong time, Bill Gordon embarrassed his mother.

   Predicate nominative: His favorite occupation was boning chucks at Camp's Market.

4. Infinitive phrase as a noun: <u>To live and die free</u> remains New Hampshire's motto.

   Infinitive phrase as an adjective: A simple decision <u>to appoint a Republican to the Board of Education</u> resulted in civil turmoil.

   Infinitive phrase as an adverb: Bob chastised the student <u>to teach her a lesson</u>.

Task 13

Page 37, Chapter 4, Clauses, Identifying restrictive or nonrestrictive clauses

1. This sentence needs commas around the clause "who wrote such works as *Affliction* and *Continental Drift,*" a nonessential clause.

2. This sentence needs commas around "who coached in the NBA," a nonessential clause.

3. Do not use commas; otherwise, the sense of the sentence changes. The dependent clause is essential to the sentence.

4. No commas are needed because "who sang in the competition last Friday" is essential to the sentence.

5. Again, no commas are needed. The clause "who applied to colleges early this year" is essential to the sentence.

6. Use commas after "Riccio" and after "school" because this clause, beginning with "who," is not essential to the sentence.

7. C

8. C Perhaps the word "that" should be used in place of "which."

9. C

10. It is best to rewrite this one: The student who ranked as the most likeable child at St. John's School was Caroline Fitzgerald, who also had fourteen "A's" on her report card.

Task 14

Pages 38–39, Chapter 4, Clauses, Identifying the clauses and their functions

1. *Whatever Lola wants*—noun, direct object of "gets"

2. *Before he enlisted in the Marines*—adverb, modifying "hunted"

3. *who were delighted with their offspring*—adjective, modifying "parents"; *that I would become a schoolteacher*—noun, direct object of "decided"

4. *Whenever Elizabeth Ann McGuinness and John James McGuinness go on a long bus trip*—adverb, modifying "take"; *which help them with their ennui*—adjective, modifying "books"

5. *whoever praised his schoolwork*—noun, object of the preposition "to"

6. *who was the sports editor of the* New Haven Register, *who gave Albie Booth the nickname of "Little Boy Blue"*—both adjectives modifying "Mulvey"

7. *Whatever bid Gerd Nelson makes while playing bridge*—noun, subject of "pleases"

8. *While he was vacationing in Florida*—adverb, modifying "caught"; *which he sold to local fish stores*—adjective, modifying "grouper"

9. *After the World Trade Center buildings fell*—adverb, modifying "changed"; *that we had known*—adjective, modifying "way of life"

10. *where they were at the time of the tragedy*—noun, direct object of "remember"

Task 15

Pages 39–40, Chapter 4, Clauses, Reviewing Chapters 3 and 4

1. *For some weeks now*

2. *dispersing the contents of this apartment*

3. *trying to persuade hundreds of inanimate objects to scatter and leave me alone*

4. *to persuade hundreds of inanimate objects*

5. *that some morning, as if by magic, all books, pictures, records, chairs, beds, curtains, lamps, china, glass, utensils, keepsakes would drain away from around my feet*

6. *Even after he had departed with his heavy load*

7. *to empty the place completely, to be almost as many books as before*

8. *exploding in the living room like a bomb, detonated by his grief*

Task 16

Page 40, Chapter 4, Clauses, Reviewing Chapters 3 and 4. The sentences that follow are suggestions only:

1. *In her haste*, Carley Davis forgot the food for the picnic.

2. *After the Yankee game with Tampa Bay*, Erin, Quippy, and I took the last train to New Haven.

3. *Frogs* Mack and the boys love to hunt because the slimy green things were like currency at Lee Chong's in Cannery Row.

4. *Beginning next week*, school busses in Madison will be equipped with television monitors.

5. *Fighting off tacklers* might be the most difficult task for an offensive lineman.

6. *To end a conversation without some closure* is considered rude.

7. *Since Matt Gentile has become a lawyer*, he has won every case presented to him.

8. *Whoever scores the first touchdown in an NFL game* usually wins the contest.

9. Eileen and Gunnar Johnson, *who present clinics on dancing*, find humor in almost everything.

10. The man *whom I met at the Durham Fair* turned out to be the mayor of East Hartford.

Task 17

Page 46, Chapter 5, The Verb, Rewriting the passive voice

1. Often at the afternoon movies, the ushers noticed the young man in the blue suit.

2. The signs at West Wharf, until now, instructed fishermen to pick up after themselves.

3. If you have permission to drive your parents' car, you should learn the rules of the road.

4. I took my cat to the vet's because it had a golf ball sized tick bite.

5. The administration told the teachers that it was extending the school year two months with no summer vacation.

6. Officials of Metro North gave extra bonuses to the conductors even though many trains were not running.

7. The tenants of the old house had the heat turned up to the highest setting, but they still froze because the heat leaked through the dilapidated shutters.

8. In 2000, The Texas Rangers signed Alex Rodriguez to the biggest contract ever received at that point, by a Major League player.

9. The owner of Malone's instructs the wait staff to consider the customer first.

10. My students gave me a computer.

Task 18

Page 49, Chapter 5, The Verb, Determining linking and active verbs

1. *smelled*—active
2. *looked*—linking
3. *remained*—active
4. *became*—linking
5. *tasted*—active
6. *felt*—linking
7. *appeared*—active
8. *stayed*—linking
9. *grew*—linking
10. *brought*—active

Task 19

Page 56, Chapter 5, The Verb, Changing passive verbs to active verbs

1. . . . and her employees recognized her as a model citizen...
2. C
3. The teacher kept Josh Stone . . .
4. . . . earned the distinction as Nurse of the Year, . . .
5. If Woody were . . .
6. . . . was the one . . .
7. . . . that I made . . .
8. Many consider Barack Obama to be one of . . . but others think he is too young . . .
9. . . . if he stayed . . .
10. Playing Spider Solitaire wastes time, running benefits my health, and donating to charities fulfills my soul.

Review of Chapters 1–5

Pages 57–58, Chapter 6, Paragraph from *Great Books* by David Denby

1. J
2. D
3. E
4. E
5. E
6. F
7. G
8. J
9. I
10. A
11. I
12. C
13. C, H
14. C
15. D
16. A
17. J
18. A
19. K
20. K
21. I
22. A

Review of Chapters 1–5

Pages 58–59, Chapter 6, Paragraph from *Daisy Miller* by Henry James

1. A, adverb, modifying "were"
2. A, adjective, modifying "way"

3. A, adjective, modifying "gate"

4. J, modifying "were"

5. H

6. L

7. N

8. B

9. D

10. Q

11. I, noun (or pronoun)

12. I, direct object

13. C

14. D

15. K

16. J

17. A The first one is an adjective; the second also is an adjective.

18. A, adjective

19. J

20. J

21. G

22. A, adverb

23. A, adverb

24. P

25. K

26. I, subject

27. J

28. N

29. J

30. R

31. J

32. P

33. E

34. K

35. I, direct object

36. E

37. J

38. O

39. H

40. D

Task 20

Pages 63–64, Chapter 7, Types of Sentences, Identifying sentences by type

1. Complex

2. Compound-complex

3. Complex

4. Simple

5. Compound

6. Compound-complex

7. Complex

8. Complex

9. Compound

10. Compound-complex

Note: Babe Ruth hit 29 home runs in World Series games; 714, regular season.

Task 21

Pages 68–69, Chapter 8, Coordination and Subordination, Deciding to coordinate or subordinate

1. *While Reverend Arthur Dimmesdale tortured himself over his sins, Hester Prynne changed the significance of the scarlet "A" from "Adultress" to "Angel."* Since Hester is in the main clause, the writer here emphasizes that she indeed is the more important character. This next writer feels that the two characters' torment was of

the same degree although contrasted: *Reverend Arthur Dimmesdale tortured himself over his sins; however, Hester Prynne changed the significance. . . .*

2. *Although Mike Piazza helped the Mets offensively but not defensively, Al Leiter added defensive power and clubhouse spirit to the pitching staff.* Here, the writer implies that Lieter was more valuable to the club. The next writer seems to be talking mostly plusses: *Mike Piazza helped the Mets . . . ; moreover, Al Leiter added. . . .*

3. *Choosing a computer ranks . . . beginner, and adding needed programs. . . .* Here, the author intends both thoughts to be important. This next author subordinates the first clause, and that subordination places emphasis on the second clause: *While choosing a computer . . . beginner, adding needed programs. . . .*

4. *Educators every five years propose earthshaking plans, but taxpayers usually have no voice in the matter.* Here is a compound sentence making both clauses equal with proper relationship shown by "but." Some writers might want to stress the relationship more with the following: *Educators every five years . . . ; however, taxpayers. . . .*

5. I would write the second clause as it is and end the sentence this way: *. . . in detail, showing that harvesting swordfish demands . . . .*

6. Here is an example where the writer might want to change the second clause into a phrase: *A student using J. I. Rodale's* The Synonym Finder *or one of the thesauri can always find help with vocabulary.*

7. This pair of simple sentences can easily be coordinated: *. . . , but being studious . . . teenagers.* But it can also be subordinated: *Although being cool . . . , being studious. . . .*

8. Both of these simple sentences seem to demand coordination: *The Irish economy . . . ; for example, more computers . . . country.*

9. Again, coordination is in order: *. . . owners; however, cars. . . .*

10. Here's the way old timers would revise: *Players today set records with the amount of salary received, but Babe Ruth at his best earned only eighty thousand dollars for one year.*

Task 22

Pages 72–73, Chapter 9, Reference of Pronouns, Finding reference of pronoun mistakes

1. D   A "few" what? Exchange "baseballs" or "home run balls" so that there is no more weak reference.

2. B   "Which" is generally referring to something the tour guide had said. This sentence must be revised: Our tour guide made some tourists on the trip angry when he said negative things about Americans.

3. C

4. A   "They" and "their" seems to refer to both "rights" and "anglers." Revision: Unless they stand up for their rights, recreational anglers may lose impact on politicians.

5. E   In the paper the other day, the editor announced. . . . Getting rid of the pronoun is best.

6. B   "That" refers generally to a number of ideas. Suggested revision: . . . *dollars. These statistics made me. . . .*

7. C   The teacher has already been identified as feminine. The pupil is the antecedent of the masculine pronoun.

8. B   "It" refers generally. Revision: *Because the rain continued for several days, I found activities indoors.*

9. A   "They" is ambiguous referring to both "students" and "busses." Either repeat the word "busses" and eliminate "they," or revise completely.

10. B   "It" refers generally to the idea of the ball being altered. Suggested revision: *The pitcher's rubbing the baseball with resin caused the next pitch to drop sharply into the strike zone.*

Task 23

Pages 73–74, Chapter 9, Reference of Pronouns, Reviewing Chapters 8 and 9

1. B   To correct the incorrect subordination, use "if" instead of "although."

2. A   Ambiguous reference because "they" refers to both "transparencies" and "points." Suggested revision: *Even though they help the presenter clarify some technical points, transparencies are difficult to use.*

3. C   Good sports trivia, also.

4. A   Ambiguous reference because "it" refers to both the ship and the berg. Suggested revision: Replace "it" with "ship."

5. A   General reference because "which" refers generally to the idea of the bargain. Suggested revision: *Season ticket holders rejoiced when officials of MSG announced a reduction in price.*

6. B   Incorrect coordination because the sentence needs "but," not "and."

7. A Ambiguous because "he" refers to both Twain and Harte. Suggested revision: *Bret Harte would get roaring drunk and smoke all the cigars in the house when he visited with Mark Twain in Hartford.*

8. C

9. B Incorrect coordination because "but" is needed in place of "and."

10. A Indefinite use of pronoun but probably acceptable in informal speech. Suggested revision: *A rarity occurs when my uncle lets me use his boat.*

Task 24

Page 79, Chapter 10, Agreement, Correcting agreement problems

1. "Demand" does not agree with the subject "psychology." Use "demands."

2. Correct

3. "Was" should be "were" because "replicas" is plural.

4. "Were" should be "was" because "refuge" is singular

5. Correct

6. "Their" should be "his"; to avoid sexist language, change "Every Senator" to "All Senators."

7. A plural subject demands a plural verb. Change "dominates" to "dominate."

8. "kind" should be "kinds" to agree with the verb "are."

9. "blows" should be "blow" because "none" is plural because of "leaves."

10. "attack" should be "attacks" to agree with "Ahab." The intervening phrase does not affect the number of the verb.

11. "provides" should be "provide" to agree with "Some," which is plural because of "passages."

Task 25

Page 80, Chapter 10, Agreement, Reviewing Chapters 8–10

1. D Since "moratoria" is plural, the verb must be "have."

2. C "Which" refers generally to a bunch of facts.

3. C Indefinite use of the word "They."

4. A

5. D   "Baffles" would be the choice because "Physics" is considered singular.

6. D   "Their" should be "he" or "she" because "everyone" is singular.

7. B   "Moreover" causes incorrect coordination; "however" is the better choice.

8. A

9. D   "he" refers to both Gerry and the student.

10. A

Task 26

Pages 87–88, Chapter 11, Parallel Structure, Correcting parallel structure mistakes

1. Emily Dickinson wrote beautiful poetry not only <u>about nature</u> but also <u>about love</u>, even though she rarely left her home or was attached to anyone.

2. Correct

3. *The Marble Faun* by Hawthorne is both <u>a riveting murder mystery</u> and <u>an excellent travel guide</u> through parts of Italy.

4. <u>Fishing on the bottom for tautag</u> is more exciting than <u>trolling for bluefish on top</u>.

5. . . . because no one really understood the premise and because his agents . . . (Notice in the original sentence that there is an adverb clause paired with a sentence. By adding "because" to the sentence, the correction shows now two adverb clauses.)

6. Casting for striped bass requires a knowledge of the local waters, demands certain equipment, and beckons anglers at early hours when the bass are feeding.

7. . . . and bemoans the fact that she never met her famous grandfather. (The purist corrects this sentence. The other states that the sentence is correct even though there are two tenses involved.)

8. . . . recipes, and, in general, know-it-alls.

9. In this sentence, change "exploring" to "explore," and "telling" to "tell."

10. . . . and that I would get two free tickets . . .

Task 27

Pages 88–89, Chapter 11, Parallel Structure, Reviewing previous chapters

1. D   The word "golf balls" is missing, a case of weak reference.

2. E   We need to move "not only" before the word "represents."

3. A

4. A

5. C   If both are male, we have an ambiguous reference problem. Getting rid of the pronoun will correct the error.

6. D   Again, getting rid of the pronoun will correct this sentence. Drop "they have" and replace "committed" with "committing."

7. A   Hard-hearted as it sounds.

8. E   "Illustrating" should be changed to "an illustrator of."

9. B   Use "and" not "but."

10. D   "Anyone" is singular, but the rest of the pronouns are plural. Change "anyone" to "applicants."

11. D   "have" should be "has" because the subject is singular and not affected by the intervening phrase.

12. A

13. C   "which" refers generally to a bunch of ideas. Change "which makes" to "These facts make" and place a period after "roam."

14. A

15. E   Add "by" just before "anyone" to make these sentence elements parallel.

Task 28

Page 92, Chapter 12, Misplaced and Dangling Modifiers, Identifying misplaced or dangling modifiers

1. Dangling—"Based on . . . client" does not modify "lawyer" or anything else sensibly. Correction: *The lawyer assumed the other party was guilty because of the circumstantial evidence favoring his client.*

2. Misplaced—"For facial takes" does not modify "mirror." Correction: *Rehearsing his difficult role, in front of a mirror the actor practiced for facial takes.*

3. Correct

4. Misplaced—Correction: *In an hour, the professional photographer took pictures of everyone who walked by.*

5. Dangling—Correction: *As the SST approached the runway on the outer portion eastward, the control tower ordered the pilot to abandon the landing and try again.*

6. Misplaced—Correction: *Around the house, most anglers have at least one broken rod that could be converted into an ice fishing jigging rod.*

7. Correct

8. Dangling—Correction: *The chores that bother me the most are emptying the garbage or washing the kitchen floor.*

9. I would say correct, but "their" is incorrect. In baseball lingo, this sentence is definitely a "change-up" because it shows an agreement problem—not a misplaced or dangling modifier.

10. Correct

Task 29

Pages 92–93, Chapter 12, Misplaced and Dangling Modifiers, Correcting coordination and subordination, reference of pronoun errors, agreement problems, and parallel structure errors and finding misplaced and dangling modifiers.

1. A   Booth made the kick and defeated Army that day. (The sentence was written in 1939, in the *New Haven Register*, by my father, Daniel F. X. Mulvey, Sports Editor.)

2. D   "They" has to be "he."

3. C   To clear this general reference problem up, we need to add a few words: "the price of" before "which" does the trick.

4. F   The teacher on duty reprimanded the frolicking youngster for being reckless.

5. D   The verb should be "was."

6. D   The verb does not agree with the subject. "Gam" needs "was" as its verb.

7. E   Jack Davis, who is not only a world recognized psychiatrist but also an accomplished artist, ran the Grove School in Madison, Connecticut.

8. F   Near the supermarket as he ran along the last mile of the six mile race in the town of Biloxi, Larry O'Shea Jr. felt a pang in his side.

9. A

10. A

11. D   "Plans" (singular) should be used because "Diane Wiknik Andrews" is singular.

12. A

13. D and B   "Is" should be "are" because "things" is plural; then, "and" must be "but" to coordinate things properly.

14. C

15. A

Task 30

Pages 95–96, Chapter 13, Sentence Variety, Writing sentences according to directions

1. Hank and Johanne Maguire regale their house guests with piano concertos by Mozart. (compound subject, but one verb = simple sentence)

2. Britt Evalena Henriksson Worthington runs the Boston Marathon every year, <u>but</u> she avoids the New York Marathon every other year. (two main clauses separated by <u>a comma and a conjunction</u>)

3. [Every spring, Robert F. Schumann travels to Maine] <u>because he navigates his Hinkley "picnic boat" from Down East to Connecticut.</u> ([one main clause], <u>one subordinate clause</u>)

4. [Marjorie Mitchell Maguire, <u>whose name is an example of alliteration</u>, lives in Killingworth]; [years ago she resided in Pine Orchard, Connecticut.] ([two main clauses] and <u>one dependent clause</u>)

5. <u>In the morning</u>, Marilyn Schumann swims from Clam Rock to Tuxis Island. (prepositional phrase "In the morning" begins the sentence)

6. <u>For several weeks during the middle of the summer</u>, Bob and Tina Williams make a run for Shelter Island. (three prepositional phrases beginning the sentence)

7. <u>Beautiful sentences</u> Jeremy Keim wrote for every assignment. (direct object at the beginning of the sentence)

8. <u>Cruising at forty knots</u>, Bob Williams thrills his children Dax, Cory, Alianna, Ampara, and Giana. (participial phrase at the beginning)

9. <u>Living here and in London</u> keeps Richard and Gloria Gibbons hopping. (gerund phrase used as the subject)

10. <u>Whoever ran into Annie Chase Galle's car</u> did not identify himself. (noun clause as the subject)

11. <u>Energetic</u>, Dr. K. J. Lee delivered a lecture in Dublin, Ireland. (single adjective at the beginning of the sentence)

12. <u>Caring and beautiful</u>, Carolyn Ann Eltzholtz makes everyone feel important. (two adjectives set off by commas and separated by a coordinating conjunction)

13. <u>Stealthily</u>, John Eltzholtz stashed the bushel of clams underneath the rug at Quippy's. (single adverb set off by a comma)

14. <u>Quietly</u> and <u>carefully</u>, Julie Christina Votto directed the elderly lady back to Room 40. (two adverbs joined by a coordinating conjunction)

15. <u>After they celebrated the holidays on Nantucket,</u> Jacey Nicole Votto and Mary Beth Simmons treated their parents to Disney World. (sentence beginning with an adverb clause)

16. <u>To aggravate the neighbors fully,</u> Paul Davis and Bob Brickley added an extra charge to the Admiralty Club cannon. (infinitive phrase beginning the sentence)

17. Answers here will vary.

Review Test of Chapters 2–13

Pages 97–99, Chapter 14

1. J   Correction: *The administration told Michael James Rode that he had been selected. . . .*

2. D   To make things parallel, eliminate "she" in the last clause.

3. C   Use "but" not "and."

4. J   Joan Teri Rode's classmates chose her not only. . . .

5. L, H   First, a semicolon after "injection" clears up the run-on. But the sequence of tenses demands the present perfect: . . . he thought he might have been granted . . .

6. E   "Priscilla Rich" is the subject. The verb, however, is plural but should not be affected by the intervening phrase "along with . . . Cynthia." "Rides" is the correct verb.

7. GI   Very ambiguous because both "he" and "him" are unclear. Rewrite this sentence with different pronouns. Correction: *Clay Rich told his former boss, "You're going to drive me crazy."*

8. H   The subjunctive is needed here. Change "is" to "be."

9. A

10. F   "Everyone" is singular, but "they" is plural. To avoid sexism, rewrite the sentence using the plural: If smokers gave up their nasty habit, they. . . .

11. B, J   The modifier dangles here. "To show absurdity at its utmost" modifies "Nancy Bennett," but it should modify the "police officer" who is missing from the sentence. By the revision, the passive voice is eliminated. Rewrite: *To show absurdity at its utmost, the young police officer took Nancy Bennett to the police station for fingerprinting and a mugshot—all because the was a warrant for her arrest for letting her dog roam.*

12. I   "Whom" must be changed to "who" because that word is the subject of "would be."

13. GIV   "Which" refers to an idea, not to a specific word. Revise: *When old Larry O'Shea cut the lawn twice on Thursday, his boss rejoiced.*

14. K   This fragment needs a *sentence* to attach itself to. Correction: *Although Margaret Clark MacGruer thought that all the preparations for her husband's* birthday party had been accomplished, <u>she had forgotten to invite the guests</u>.

15. L, GIII   A comma is needed before "but"; the last clause, "there were none" also needs help. Instead of trying to stretch these thoughts into a compound sentence, a simple sentence will do. Correction: *Ryan Dolan found no excitement at the carnival.*

16. A   He did, too.

17. C   "Moreover" does not coordinate properly. "However" fits the bill.

18. B   The "snake" is jogging here. Revise: *A snake suddenly darted from the side of the road and frightened Kathleen Sullivan while she was jogging near Fence Creek.*

19. D   When Erin Sullivan was an eighth grader, she was chosen both as a hall monitor and a chief board eraser.

20. GI   Too many "she's" And we do not know if the teacher is female. Revise: *Kathy G. Dolan, while discussing her teacher's upcoming trip to Budapest, told Mrs. Lietze she would see a great deal in three days.*

21. L   After "advertisements" we could do the following: A. *advertisements;* or B. *advertisements, and* or C. *advertisements; amazingly, in . . .* or D. Make two sentences.

22. A

23. I   The "I" should be "me." Objective case is called for.

24. GII   Indefinite use if the word "It." Revise: *The warning on cigarette packs identifies smoking as dangerous to one's health.*

25. A

Usage Test Answers

Pages 113–115, Chapter 15

1. Change "brought" to "taken."

2. "Amount" should be "number" because "restaurants" is plural.

3. "Inferred" should be "implied." Thelma is speaking and therefore must be "implying."

4. "Effected" should be "affected." Notice how "influenced" fits here.

5. C

6. "Should of" should be "should have."

7. "Less" should be "fewer" because "mudslides" is plural.

8. "Bring" should be "take" because Jean is "going."

9. C

10. "Because" is superfluous and wrong because of "reason." Substitute "that" for "because."

11. "Less" should be "fewer" because "lambs" is plural.

12. "Like" should be "As" because a clause is being introduced.

13. "Amount" should be "number" because "donuts" is plural.

14. "Illusion" should be "allusion" because Luis is making a casual reference here.

15. "Alright" is not a word. "All right" is the proper form.

16. "Beside" should be "besides."

17. "In" has to be changed to "into."

18. "Lay" should be "lie."

19. C

20. C

21. "Because" should be eliminated or replaced with "that."

22. C

23. The "a" is superfluous.

24. Do not use "when" in a definition. In this case, we have to revise the sentence: ". . . is a ball hit just over the infielders' heads, dropping in front of the outfielders."

25. "Except" must be changed to "accept."

Task 31

Pages 149–150, Chapter 19, A Handbook of Mechanics—Punctuation and Capitalization, The Apostrophe

1. Manning's

2. parents'

3. Malone's; customers; father's

4. Unitas's

5. It's; takes

6. C

7. C (One assumes one turtle)

8. C

9. Greenlaw's

10. bags; Mars

Task 32

Page 151, Chapter 19, A Handbook of Mechanics—Punctuation and Capitalization

1. Grover Whalen, Manhattan's perennial greeter and president of New York's World's Fair, summered in Madison, Connecticut, next to the East Wharf beach.

2. During the vernal equinox, winter flounder, flatfish to the novice, begin feeding voraciously along the beaches of Long Island Sound.

3. James Thurber, on June 16, 1928, published a short story, "Advice to American Ladies," in that week's *New Yorker*.

4. C

5. Gene "Rip" Calzetta, a local barber of renown, once fell asleep on the top of a subway car in Grand Central Station.

6. "Please give the tautog to Lou Santanelli and his brother Richie before they sic the mob on you," pleaded Tim Malone.

7. C

8. Editing the copy of the new magazine, "River & Shore," Dennis Bell found several grammatical errors in the article about Cedar Island.

9. Both are correct.

10. If the Chief was disabled, why would the town grant him nearly one hundred grand? was the question on most thoughtful taxpayers' minds.

Grammar Final Answers

Pages 154–161, Chapter 21

1. (K) Needs a sentence to make this fragment valid. *In the month of May just when the weather breaks and the water temperature reaches 50 degrees, bass rush into Long Island Sound.*

2. (Q) "From birth," of course, is not needed.

3. (O, P) "the 'House That Ruth Built,' " is a nonrestrictive appositive and needs commas setting it off. Also, "acommodates" needs another "c."

4. (E, O) The intervening phrase has nothing to do with the subject and verb— "Kim Davis visits"; the comma is needed to separate "Cooperstown" from "New York."

5. (O) Two rules of the comma are violated here: "the Superintendent of Schools in Durham, Connecticut," one for the nonessential appositive and the other separating the town from the state.

6. (B, R) "When boarding the "f" train that goes to Brooklyn" does not modify "it," the subject of the main clause. Correction: *When I take the "F" Train* (no lowercase letter here) *that goes to Brooklyn, I wait for one that isn't crowded.*

7. (B) "Dressed in nothing but a nightgown" does not modify "burglar." Correction: *The burglar froze when he saw the woman dressed only in a nightgown and holding a shotgun.*

8. (M) "In" should be "into." The implication here is that he came from outside. The hush wouldn't have occurred if he were already in the room.

9. (L) Two main clauses need to be separated by something besides a comma. The conjunction "and" fits nicely.

10. (Q, M) "About his life" is superfluous; "amount" should be "number" because "people" is plural; also, "who" should be used to refer to "people."

11. (G, M) Borderline reference of pronoun error because there really are too many pronouns. "So" should not be used by itself. "That" should follow "so" for accuracy.

12. (R, I) Because the course has a number, capitals are needed for "Home Economics." The tense called for here is the past perfect to indicate a time in the past completed before some other time in the past. Therefore, "had earned. . . ."

13. (A) This was taken from a column my father wrote for the *New Haven Register* in 1931. I hope it's correct.

14. (D, E, O) "To enjoy" must follow "to frolic" for parallel structure. "Are" should be the verb because the subject is compounded by "and." Finally, the comma is not needed—never separate the subject from its verb by a comma.

15. (I) The subjunctive form is needed here. "Were" instead of "was."

16. (A) This is the first line of one of my favorite poems, "Richard Cory" by E. A. Robinson, one of my favorite poets.

17. (H) The first "I" is correct as the subject. The second should be "me" because it's the object.

18. (K) Classic fragment because it looks good enough to be a sentence. Adding "he never seems hungry" might be one way to help this fragment out.

19. (O) Comma needed after "adage" because this is a compound sentence.

20. (I) The verb tense is wrong. Present tense does not work here. Present perfect, "has been" does.

21. (M) Two usage errors: "less" should be "fewer" and "then" should be "than."

22. (B) "This year" is misplaced—actually goes two ways. Placing it at the beginning of the sentence, however, clears everything.

23. (D) . . . *Nancy Martin not only captured the hearts of her students but also reigned as the queen.* . . . Now the verbs follow the correlatives.

24. (F) "Someone" is singular, but "they" is plural: They do not agree. Best way: Get rid of the indefinite pronoun and substitute "workers," "employees," or whatever word you might choose—as long as the word is plural.

25. (E, F) "Wish" should be "wishes"; "they" and "they" should also be singular to agree with "Griffey," along with "was" instead of "were."

26. (Q) If something is "unique," then "very" is not needed.

27. (D) For the purist. "Taking pictures" is part of the gerund phrase as the subject of the first clause. Why not then start the second clause with "finding one" instead of the infinitive phrase "to find one"?

28. (A) This sentence is from Joseph Conrad.

29. (O) We need a comma after "284" because a nonessential clause follows.

30. (A) What seems amiss here is that the direct object appears first and almost reads as the subject.

31. (M) Gatling "invented" that particular type of gun.

32. (B) The clause "that discussed plans for the five-year mission to rebuild the program" should be placed next to "Committee."

33. (A) This sentence is from Lord Byron.

34. (R) Of course, capitalize "Empire State Building" and "Central Park."

35. (R) "blues singer"

36. (O) A nonrestrictive appositive needs commas—before "where" and after "world."

37. (N) A question mark is needed after the conductor's question. A comma is needed after "thirty" in the passenger's response.

38. (S) "You" should be changed to "they" because a writer should not go from third person to second person—it damages the sentence's transmission.

39. (C) "Subsequently" means "later" and just does not convey the transition needed. "Consequently" seems to fit the bill.

40. (K) After "see" a verb phrase is needed since "driving" is the subject of this thought. Perhaps "rattles most first time drivers" might suffice. Also, add a comma after "see."

41. (P) For some reason, "paraphernalia" is difficult for 99 percent of the population to spell.

42. (M) "These kinds" or "This kind" clears up this usage error.

43. (B) In a box labeled "FRAGILE" should begin the sentence and alleviate the misplacement.

44. (L) This run-on is really confusing. Something must be inserted between "meeting" and "the name." Possibilities include: A. placing a semicolon; B. making two sentences; C. using a comma and "but"; and D. using a semicolon and "however" and then a comma.

45. (G) or (B) You have a choice of errors. "Which" seems to refer generally to the rest of the sentence. Also, the "which" clause is misplaced and therefore should be moved.

46. (A) No comma needed after 1947 because there is no confusion by omitting it.

47. (H) "I" *sounds* correct. "Me" is correct because it's the object of the preposition "for."

48. (H) Very common to mix up "whoever" and "whomever." Since it is the subject of the adjective clause, "whoever" is called for.

49. (M) "Like" should be "as if." "There is no tomorrow" is a clause and cannot be introduced with "like."

50. (B, P) "Taking no chances" dangles. Obviously this participial phrase modifies those with the needles. Also, "inoculated" is the correct spelling. This is one of those sentences that must be rewritten: Taking no chances Dr. Flanagan decided to inoculate the children at the Jeffrey Elementary School.

51. (A) This is the last line from one of Macbeth's soliloquies. I would not argue with Shakespeare.

52. (K) After "television" there must be something added. "Nothing significant happened" might do.

53. (O) One time my daughter and I, during a return flight from Los Angeles, saw Jack Kramer, the 1947 Men's Singles Champion at Wimbledon, walk by us. I inserted the commas; I also grabbed his autograph.

54. (A) This sentence is from the Constitution.

55. (D) Eliminate "she." Then the correlative conjunctions fall into place.

56. (E) "Does" should be "do" to agree with the compound subject.

57. (C, O) "And" does not coordinate, but "but" does. Also, a comma is needed before "but."

58. (N, O) *Aram Khachaturian, although not well known, is famous for* Gavane, *a ballet, and from that work, of course, "Sabre Dance," a song that is recognizable.*

59. (I) It still is.

60. (T) If the word "other" is not added after "any," there would be a comparison error.

61. (E) "Plants" and "prays" agree with Gerald Birnbaum, even though Jay, his wife, does not.

62. (I, M) "Cast" is the correct past participle, and "accept" should be "except."

63. (C) Use "but," not "and."

64. (P) "Misspelled," "questionnaire," and "enrollment."

65. (B) "In Ireland" in the original sentence makes the strike happening only in Ireland. "In Ireland" should go at the beginning of the sentence.

66. (F, G) Either way, "one" refers to "cabinet" or does not agree with "tablets." Besides, one usually takes two—aspirin, that is—for a headache.

67. (M) The "a" is superfluous.

68. (H) "I" again *sounds* correct, but "me" is correct because "me" is the object of the preposition.

69. (J, D) With two active verbs already showing, the third should be active also. Instead of "was" substitute "participated as." Now there are three active verbs *and* parallel structure.

70. (A) The grave is in the middle of nowhere.

71. (L) After "Bull" place a comma and the conjunction "and." Or throw a semicolon after "Bull."

72. (B, K, O) Let us start at the beginning: *After a brief stop at Avis, to upgrade our car that was too small for the luggage, near Shannon Airport, on our way to Ballybunion, where a statue depicts Bill Clinton about to tee off, we stopped in Foynes for lunch.*

73. (T) There are only two players here and therefore "better" should be used for the comparative.

74. (G, R) No caps needed for "secretary of state" since there is no name attached to it. "Speaker" and "House" go with the name, and "President," when referring to the

Commander-in-Chief, is capitalized. "He" is ambiguous and must be removed in favor of the person's name.

75. (E, M) Change "stuns" to agree with "One," and "amount" should be "number" because "hot dogs" is plural.

76. (D, E) Use "are" because there is a compound subject; "to formulate" polishes off the parallel structure; and change "goal" to "goals."

77. (I, M) "Brung" must be "brought." Having said that, now we must change "brought" to "took." Remember the differences between "bring" and "take"?

78. (A) This sentence is from Charles Dickens. The man could write!

79. (B, O) *At Ohio State in basketball, Frank Howard, who also played Major League Baseball, set a rebounding record at the Holiday Festival in New York.*

80. (C) "Although" is not the word called for. "Because" is the proper subordination.

81. (F) "Their" should be "his" (or "her"). The interesting implication here, though, is that all "culprits" are male.

82. (O) Commas are needed after items in an address: *Serafino, 382 Percival Avenue, Kensington, Connecticut.* After the state comes the zip code. There usually is no comma between zip codes and states.

83. (A) This wonderful, correct, poetic sentence is from Matthew Arnold.

84. (P) Ukulele, separately. There might be a question of "they" referring to band. "They" is okay if you are thinking of them as individuals.

85. (A) This is from Emily Dickinson. I would not argue with her unless she would agree that a semicolon should be placed after "church."

86. (G) The pronoun "they" is ambiguous. Even if we add "whales," we still need to recast the sentence, eliminating the pronouns: *Many whalers thought whales ubiquitous because certain leviathans had been seen in different parts of the world at the same time.* (No radios then)

87. (N) A semicolon is needed after "problems."

88. (A)

89. (G) "Which" refers generally to the statement before. What made many residents panic? The program done away with? The lack of funds? The sentence should be revised: *When the industrial arts program at the high school was cancelled because of low funding, many residents were alarmed.*

90. (R) No capitals for "nineteen hundreds" or "two thousands." Doesn't the second one sound strange to say?

91. (M) "As" should be "like."

92. (E or M) "Data" is plural. The verb then must be "are" rather than "is." Or change "data" to "datum." "Data," however, is the more logical choice.

93. (M) "Accepted" must be "excepted" because the sense of the word means to leave out.

94. (A) This sentence was written by Sir Francis Bacon.

95. (R) "New" must be capitalized.

96. (F) Since "participant" is singular, "their" must be changed to "his" or "her." To avoid the sexism, change "participant" to "participants."

97. (I) "Went" is the past tense of "go." We need the past participle, "gone."

98. (N) The colon should be changed to a semicolon because the second main clause does not explain the first main clause.

99. (A) Notice the active verbs.

100. (L) The comma after "Board of Education" should be a semicolon.

A2

Appendix 2: A List of Prepositions

about	beyond	over	according to
above	by	since	because of
across	down	through	by way of
after	during	throughout	in addition to
against	except	till	in front of
among	for	to	in place of
around	from	toward	in regard to
as	in	under	in spite of
at	inside	until	instead of
athwart	into	up	on account of
before	like	upon	out of
behind	near	with	with regard to
below	of	without	
beneath	off		
beside	on		
besides	out		
between	outside		

Appendix 3: A Partial List of Irregular Verbs

With special thanks to Kay Mastin Mallory, English-Zone.Com Teacher (*english-zone.com*). Definitely check out the Web site.

Present	Past Tense	Past Participle	Present Participle
arise	arose	arisen	arising
awake	awoke or awaked	awoken or awaked	awaking
bear	bore	borne	bearing
beat	beat	beaten	beating
become	became	become	becoming
begin	began	begun	beginning
bend	bent	bent	bending
bet	bet or betted	bet or betted	betting
bind	bound	bound	binding
bite	bit	bitten or bit	biting
bleed	bled	bled	bleeding
blow	blew	blown	blowing
break	broke	broken	breaking
breed	bred	bred	breeding
build	built	built	building
buy	bought	bought	buying
catch	caught	caught	catching
choose	chose	chosen	choosing
cling	clung	clung	clinging
come	came	come	coming
creep	crept	crept	creeping
cut	cut	cut	cutting
deal	dealt	dealt	dealing
dig	dug	dug	digging
dive	dived or dove	dived	diving
do	did	done	doing
drag	dragged	dragged	dragging

Present	Past Tense	Past Participle	Present Participle
draw	drew	drawn	drawing
dream	dreamed or dreamt	dreamed or dreamt	dreaming
drink	drank	drunk	drinking
drive	drove	driven	driving
drown	drowned	drowned	drowning
eat	ate	eaten	eating
fall	fell	fallen	falling
feed	fed	fed	feeding
feel	felt	felt	feeling
fight	fought	fought	fighting
find	found	found	finding
flee	fled	fled	fleeing
fling	flung	flung	flinging
fly	flew	flown	flying
forbid	forbade	forbidden	forbidding
forget	forgot	forgot	forgetting
forgive	forgave	forgiven	forgiving
freeze	froze	frozen	freezing
get	got	gotten or got	getting
give	gave	given	giving
go	went	gone	going
grind	ground	ground	grinding
grow	grew	grown	growing
hang	hung	hung	hanging (suspending)
hang	hanged	hanged	hanging (from a rope)
have	had	had	having
hear	heard	heard	hearing
hide	hid	hidden	hiding
hold	held	held	holding
hurt	hurt	hurt	hurting
keep	kept	kept	keeping
know	knew	known	knowing
lay	laid	laid	laying
lead	led	led	leading
leave	left	left	leading
lend	lent	lent	lending
let	let	let	letting
lie	lay	lay	lying
lose	lost	lost	losing
make	made	made	making

Present	Past Tense	Past Participle	Present Participle
mean	meant	meant	meaning
meet	met	met	meeting
pay	paid	paid	paying
prove	proved	proven	proving
put	put	put	putting
putt	putted	putted	putting
quit	quit	quit	quitting
read	read	read	reading
ride	rode	rode	riding
ring	rang	rung	ringing
rise	rose	risen	rising
run	ran	run	running
saw	sawed	sawn	sawing
say	said	said	saying
see	saw	seen	seeing
seek	sought	sought	seeking
sell	sold	sold	selling
send	sent	sent	sending
set	set	set	setting
shake	shook	shaken	shaking
shed	shed	shed	shedding
shine	shone or shined	shone or shined	shining
shoe	shod	shod	shoeing
shoot	shot	shot	shooting
show	showed	showed or shown	showing
shrink	shrank or shrink	shrunk or shrunken	shrinking
shut	shut	shut	shutting
sing	sang	sung	singing
sink	sank	sunk	sinking
sit	sat	sat	sitting
slay	slew	slew	slaying
sleep	slept	slept	sleeping
slide	slid	slid	sliding
sling	slung	slung	slinging
speak	spoke	spoken	speaking
spend	spent	spent	spending
spin	spun	spun	spinning
spread	spread	spread	spreading
spring	sprang	sprung	springing
stand	stood	stood	standing

Present	Past Tense	Past Participle	Present Participle
steal	stole	stolen	stealing
stick	stuck	stuck	sticking
sting	stung	stung	stinging
stink	stank or stink	stunk	stinking
strike	struck	struck or stricken	striking
string	strung	strung	stringing
strive	strove	striven	striving
swear	swore	sworn	swearing
sweep	swept	swept	sweeping
swim	swam	swum	swimming
swing	swung	swung	swinging
take	took	taken	taking
teach	taught	taught	teaching
tear	tore	torn	tearing
tell	told	told	telling
think	thought	thought	thinking
throw	threw	thrown	throwing
tread	trod	trodden	treading
wake	woke	waken	waking
wear	wore	worn	wearing
understand	understood	understood	understanding
win	won	won	winning
wind	wound	wound	winding
wring	wrung	wrung	wringing
write	wrote	written	writing

Appendix 4:
Bits and Pieces

FROM THE NEW HAVEN REGISTER, SATURDAY, OCTOBER 13, 2001

"Police responded to reports of gunfire at about 9 p.m. At least 50 shots were fired by automatic weapons in what police believe was a conflagration between two rival factions." Where was the fire department?

ANSWERS TO QUESTIONS FROM PRONOUN SECTION

1. Willie Mays was on deck.
2. Hoyt Wilhelm hit a home run his first at bat in the Major Leagues; he played in over a thousand more games without hitting another one. He was known not only as a great knuckleball pitcher but also as a notoriously poor hitter.

REDUNDANCY

Seen in a restaurant window: "Now open 7 days a week, Mon tru [sic] Sun".

MISPLACED MODIFIERS

From *The New York Times*, Sunday, March 25, 2000, Caption under a picture of ostriches: "There is a huge demand for ostrich meat <u>from Europe</u>, with its disease-ravaged meat industry." (Author's underline points out a huge misplaced modifier!)

Two misplaced modifiers appeared in the same article (*The Source*, Madison, Connecticut, April 12, 2001, in an article about The Leatherman).

1. "Exactly who was Jules Bourglay and how did he end up dead in a cave <u>dressed entirely in leather</u>?" Singular cave!

2. "His shoes were of cyclopean proportions: soles of thick wood, rounded, with curled up toes <u>weighing ten pounds</u>." I'll bet his fingers were huge too.

GRAMMAR DISCUSSION

Gerry came up with a problem from Joan: "He spent his time walking on the beach." The question is: What sentence element is "walking on the beach"? Possibilities:

1. Participle, modifying "time"

2. Participle, modifying "He"—The sentence would read "Walking on the beach, he spent his time"; however, this version seems awkward (an English teacher's term which means "I can't quite figure this one out!")

3. Gerund in apposition to "time"

OVERHEARD

April 14, 2001, in reference to getting to the North Shore: "I have never <u>took</u> that ferry before."

WORD JOKE

Did you hear about the agnostic dyslexic insomniac? He lay awake one night wondering, "Is there really a dog?"

THE IMPORTANCE OF PUNCTUATION

The teacher (a man) wrote on the board: "A woman without her man is nothing!" Most of the young ladies in the class gasped and then some whispered audibly, "Sexist!"

When the smoke had settled, the teacher wrote underneath the first version, the same words but with different punctuation:

"A woman—without her, man is nothing!" and the jeers turned into cheers.

SPELLING STORY

In one Connecticut city just before the Roaring Twenties when horses were dragging milk wagons through the early morning streets, one of the older steeds dropped dead on Pemberton Street. The investigating officer, while writing his report at the scene, had trouble with the spelling of "Pemberton." Therefore, he and several other officers dragged the carcass over to Smith Street and there the officer finished writing his report.

BILLBOARD ADVERTISEMENT

Ringling Bros. Circus: "Nobody [singular] ever said they [plural] wanted to run away and join a video company." I don't agree either.

USAGE ERROR FROM THE CONNECTICUT DEP

Press Release, July 6, 2001, "DEP Stocks Northern Pike into Winchester Lake":
"Biologists expect that the introduction of pike will not adversely <u>effect</u> Winchester
Lake's bass population." Well, they both sound the same!

AGREEMENT IN IRELAND

During our vacation in Ireland, television watching was not one of our priorities
because in most places we could get only two channels. What I did notice was that
sports announcers of soccer games would refer to a certain country's team and then use a
plural verb with it. These are two examples that I noted:

Germany are . . .
Ukraine gather . . .

USAGE STORY

When my oldest daughter Lisa enrolled at Skidmore, the trustees of the college held a
party for the parents. I said to one of the trustees, "You're an <u>alumnus</u>?" "No," she
snapped, "I'm an <u>alumna</u>!"

NOT FOR NOTHING

I grew up with a couple of friends who would preface important announcements with
"Not for nothing," and the hairs on my arms would stand up in embarrassment. Then,
one day, Pat Williams was reading "Self-Reliance" by Ralph Waldo Emerson to her
husband, Don:

The power which resides in him (man) is new in nature, and none but he knows
what that is which he can do, nor does he know until he has tried. <u>Not for nothing</u> one
face, one character, one fact, makes much impression on him, and another none.

Hey, not for nothing, what is good enough for Emerson, is good enough for me—and
Pat and Don.

SPELLING

There are at least two American-English words that contain all the vowels, not con-
secutively, but in order: **facetious**, and **abstemious**. Any more? I just found another:
asenious—resembling or made up of or containing arsenic.

And one word, although more English than American has five vowels in a row:
queueing.

And then there's one word that has three consecutive sets of double letters: b**ookkee**ping.

ANOTHER SPELLING POSER

Ask anyone to pronounce the words you spell:

M-a-c(pause)-b-e-t-h, and he'll say "mack-beth." Then say,
M-a-c(pause)-D-o-n-a-l-d, and he'll say "mack-don-uld." Then say,
M-a-c(pause)-h-i-n-e and he'll probably say "mack-high-knee," but he should have said "muh-sheen" (machine).

FROM *MACBETH*

At the end of a soliloquy, Macbeth states: "Words to the heat of deeds too cold breath gives."

What is the subject of the sentence? "Words"? "Cold breath"? I opt for "words" even though the word does not seem to agree with the verb. Why argue with Shakespeare?

SHORT STUDENT THEME

At the beginning of the period, the teacher wrote the assignment on the board: Write an essay with the following themes: sex, religion, mystery, and royalty. You have three days for this assignment, and you may start now.

Halfway through the period a student approached the desk, complimented the teacher on the wonderful assignment, and dropped the single sheet of paper on her desk.

"Wait a minute," she said. "Do you have the four themes asked for?

"Yes, Ma'am," he smiled.

"Read it to me then," she demanded.

"Holy Moses, the Queen's pregnant. Who dunnit?"

RHYME

Is there a rhyme for "orange"? Not that I know of.

EXPLANATION OF EYE MOVEMENTS

Reading experts agree that many readers read word by word but can be trained to read many words together. Here is where a knowledge of grammar is important because the student recognizes larger sentence units rather than single words. Thus, the trained reader would see something like this:

in the middle of the night

as

inthemiddleofthenight

rather than as

in   the   middle   of   the   night

Therefore, instead of at least six eye movements, only one eye movement covers the same expanse. The result is faster reading. Reading experts say that the faster students read, the more they will comprehend. (See also page 26.)

COMPLEMENTARY OR COMPLIMENTARY?

From a local grocery flyer from Robert's Food Center in North Madison, Connecticut:

For Customers 60 Years Young And Beyond. Stop In For A Complementary Cake And Fresh Brewed Jamaican Bean Coffee In Our Food Court.

Let's see, should we mention the capitals, the misplaced modifier, or the fragment— or just the "Complementary," which should be "Complimentary." However, perhaps the cake and coffee "make up for" the mistakes.

I LOVE THE METS

I love the Mets. I love everything about them—even when they lose. I especially love the announcers Gary Cohen, Keith Hernandez, Ron Darling, Kevin Burkhardt (there is no one better), and Ralph Kiner (who brings the past alive). Of course, I love even more some of the gaffes Ron, and occasionally Keith and Gary, make.

July 9, 2008 Ron: "He (Jonathan Sanchez, pitcher SF Giants) should have went after him (Ramon Castro)." And "the older second basemens…."

July 10, 2008 "That depends on who they have on base." versus Giants, 8th inning

July 22, 2008 "Maybe he should have went with the changeup." versus Phillies, 7th inning

July 23, 2008 "If I were him…." versus Phillies, 3rd inning

August 9, 2008 (Commenting on the infielders of the Marlins with twenty or more home runs): "That's pretty unique." 2nd inning

In the same game, Gary contributed, "He (Brian Stokes) has pitched five credible innings." I know he meant creditable.

August 1, 2008 Ron, commenting on "Darling" by the Beach Boys: "…must have wore it out…." versus Pirates, 4th inning

Those slips aside, the announcing team of the Mets has no equal. On the bottom of the announcer list are Tim McCarver (see *www.shutuptimmccarver.com*), Jon Miller, and Joe Morgan.

Index

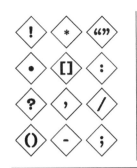

BARRON'S POCKET GUIDES—

The handy, quick-reference tools that you can count on—no matter where you are!

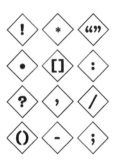

BARRON'S POCKET GUIDE CORRECT ENGLISH

Fourth Edition
Michael Temple

Sentence construction

Spelling

Punctuation

Usage

Essay and letter writing

and more

ISBN: 978-0-7641-2688-8

BARRON'S POCKET GUIDE CORRECT GRAMMAR

Fourth Edition
Vincent F. Hopper, Cedric Gale,
and Ronald C. Foote
Revised by Benjamin W. Griffith

Parts of speech

Correct usage

Review of common
grammatical errors
and how to correct them

ISBN: 978-0-7641-2690-1

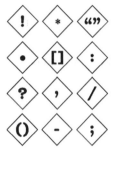

BARRON'S POCKET GUIDE THESAURUS

Second Edition
Arthur H. Bell, Ph.D.

Expanded new edition

Quick help in finding different words
with similar meanings

Includes an extensive list
of overused words

An aid to better writing style

A-to-Z format

ISBN: 978-0-7641-1995-8

BARRON'S POCKET GUIDE CORRECT SPELLING

Fourth Edition
Francis Griffith
and Mary Elizabeth

26,000 often misspelled words

Arranged alphabetically and
divided into syllables

Easy-to-remember
spelling rules

ISBN: 978-0-7641-2691-8

BARRON'S POCKET GUIDE VOCABULARY

Fourth Edition
Samuel Brownstein, Mitchel Weiner,
and Sharon Weiner Green

More than 3,000 words that
appear on SAT I and other
standardized tests

Listed alphabetically
with concise definitions
and example sentences

ISBN: 978-0-7641-2694-9

BARRON'S POCKET GUIDE STUDY TIPS

Fifth Edition
W. H. Armstrong, M. W. Lampe,
and G. Ehrenhaft

Tips for scheduling and
organizing study time

How to take useful notes

How to correct your weak points

ISBN: 978-0-7641-2693-2

BARRON'S EDUCATIONAL SERIES, INC.
250 Wireless Boulevard, Hauppauge, New York 11788
In Canada: Georgetown Book Warehouse
34 Armstrong Avenue, Georgetown, Ontario L7G 4R9

Please visit **www.barronseduc.com**
to view current prices and to order books

#18 R 3/08